CW00743236

PiROUETTE SURGERY®

Rosina Andrews

Featuring world record-holder, Sophia Lucia

Copyright © 2016 by Rosina Andrews
All rights reserved

Pirouette Surgery® is a registered trademark of Rosina Andrews.

No part of this book may be reproduced in any form or by any electronic or mechanical means including information storage and retrieval systems, without permission in writing from the author. The only exception is by a reviewer, who may quote short excerpts in a review.

Reselling through electronic outlets without the permission of the publisher is illegal and punishable by law. The scanning, uploading, and distribution of the book via the internet or any other means without the permission of the publisher is illegal and punishable by law. Please purchase only authorised editions and do not participate in or encourage electronic piracy of copyrighted material.

Your support of the author's rights is appreciated.

www.rosinaandrews.co.uk

Published by Pirouette Surgery
ISBN-13: 978-1-78280-937-1

This book is dedicated to the 'PEP' kids.

Those little dancers that trusted me,

listened to me,

and showed me that #TheUKCanTurn.

(And to all the independent London cafés that I've sat in for days on end; drinking you out of Earl Grey tea!)

CONTENTS

Introduction 7

Foreword: An Interview with Sophia Lucia 12

1. The Science of Turning 30

2. Common Faults and How to Remove Them 53

The Sellotape Phenomenon 53

The '5' Instructions 59

A T. Rex Can't Turn – Arms, Arms, Arms! 60

Upper Body Strengthening Exercises 74

Spaghetti Legs - Leg Positioning 81

Simple Leg Strengthening Exercises
Shared by Samuel Downing, Personal Trainer 88

The Goldilocks Complex! 95

Are You a Lean Backer or a Face Planter?
Posture and Core Control 107

The Wheeeeeee Factor 120

Rhythm 123

Have You Got More 'Chins' Than a Hong Kong
Telephone Directory? 129

So Close, Yet So Far 141

It's All in the Mind 145

Kicking the Habit 152

3. The Turn and its Variations   158

4. Pirouette Surgery® Ailment Chart   168

5. Adding Turning to Your Classes   175

6. Let's Talk Turns – Exclusive Interviews   180

    Krista Miller – Master Dance Coach, LA   180

    Autumn Miller – Child Star Dancer, LA   188

    Alexander Campbell – Royal Ballet Company   193

    Gabriela Banuet – Biomechanics and Pilates Master   198

    Indiana Woodward – New York City Ballet   201

    Lulu Alexandra – Champion Ice Skater   204

7. Endnote – Myra Tiffin   206

Acknowledgements   208

Bibliography   209

Index   211

INTRODUCTION

What is 'Pirouette Surgery®'? No, unfortunately it isn't a surgical operation to improve your turns, but instead, an in-depth look at the processes of teaching turns, focusing on those little niggling ailments that disrupt the consistency and success of our rotations.

This book isn't full of technical and scientific jargon. It's more accessible than that. It's a form of reference and a form of respite (for those teachers pulling their hair out, shouting the same old corrections with no result!). I will take you through my experiences of teaching turns, and with some help from my fantastic collaborators and my research results, help dancers to enhance their turns and teachers to develop their turning teaching techniques. In connection with this book is the separate teachers' manual, sharing my tried and tested Three Level Programme.

In a world where a ten-year-old can do 55 turns (I had the opportunity to meet Sophia Lucia and have included an exclusive interview in Chapter 2), hopping round on a double turn should no longer be acceptable practice. How often do we hear as teachers, 'But Maddie from *Dance Moms* does this', as our nine-year-olds in jazz classes try and nail their tricks whilst our backs are turned organising the music for a syllabus class, without any rotation exercises at all. It appears to me that turns are excluded from UK dance syllabuses until our dancers are nearly fully grown up! From my research prior to this book, the average age in the UK for starting pirouettes is 14. Why is that? There has been a lot of research lately highlighting the dangers of overstretching in young dancers, especially with over splits and acrobatic moves. We do have to be careful with young dancers' bodies but overstretching isn't something that is apparent in turning, so why do syllabuses introduce turning so late when spinning is a natural movement for younger children? Drop yourself at that Christmas party where the five-year-olds are in their glittery tights on a shiny wooden floor... cue a health and safety statement!

So, who am I and what do I know? I am a retired professional dancer, who's transitioned into teaching and choreography. Upon living in the United States for a year my perception of dance changed. The energy in the States is different from here and it is somewhere I felt at home. On arrival back in the UK, I wanted to share what I had learnt and developed a touring workshop series to expose young British dancers to new techniques and styles. In England in 2012 this was something that was still quite a new concept! (There were definitely less of us on the 'touring workshop circuit' and we hardly have any conventions like the USA.) I felt teachers were ready to share and collaborate on techniques rather than claiming sole custody of their dancers. As demands change and more versatile dancers are expected this seems only a natural progression. My successes grew and over the last three years I have travelled to over 150 different dance studios in eight different countries. Originally, my workshop, *A New York State of Mind*, delved into the contemporary side of things, developing creation and improvisation, letting dancers explore freedom of movement and pushing their boundaries by learning different choreography. Often there was a pirouette or an extension… oh I might as well just say it… a tilt… snuck into the choreography. My time in America has been and continues to be my greatest inspiration and you only have to switch on *So You Think You Can Dance* or YouTube to see how often turns feature in American choreography.

Alongside my touring workshops, on arrival back in the UK in 2012, I developed a 'Professional Extension Programme' (PEP) for my regular studio's gifted and talented students. Those that showed potential were asked to start this Saturday morning supplementary training programme, consisting of leaps and turns, body conditioning, ballet and stretch. With the advancement of social media and my following from touring workshops word soon spread as the PEP students progressed, not only was it contemporary workshops that Rosina Andrews offered, but technical focus too.

You will see selected students from the PEP programme pictured in this book and those are the children that feature on the *Three Level Programme* video clips*. From Darcie at six years old demonstrating double pirouettes; Lauren aged 12 showing us that five turns can be consistent and controlled; to Lily, signifying that at 15, turns shouldn't be something new and feared but something ingrained and shown with confidence.

*Available to access with the purchase of the teachers' manual and studio licence.

The Turn Team,
from Left to Right; Lily, Rosina, Darcie, Lauren.

But, why pirouettes? Well, I received a private message a couple of years back. *'I've been told you are the person that can make my child turn!'* Unfortunately, the follow-up of this particular child's progress never happened due to scheduling problems, however, that message sparked a confidence in me that highlighted I was doing something right and it was something that was sought after in the current UK young dancers' industry. When more and more American choreographers and companies are coming over to audition in the UK, why should we be behind on the technical tricks that for them are the basic requirements? The first round of many an American cruise company audition is often Fouettés. Are we giving British dancers the best chances if we start turns at 14 years old? When other countries offer leaps and turns classes to dancers as young as 'tiny tots'! Studios that I visited for workshops began asking for specific turning classes and so Pirouette Surgery® was born. Each year I hold an auditioned elite summer school for dancers all over the country; it's open to dancers that are at the top of their game, and Pirouette Surgery® was a hit at that workshop too! What every dancer needs, whatever their level, is to find what works for them and that there is not only one way to turn!

Don't get me wrong; it's not all about turns. There is much more to dance than tricks. I am a massive advocate of performance and musicality and I will tell any dancer, whatever style, when they ask me what they should do to improve: *'Get to another ballet class!'* Nevertheless, I am passionate about turns and felt that this book was something that would help #TheUKToTurn. I know that I also now have an American audience, so I know that you guys already turn, but I hope this book will clarify and offer some authentic new advice. With increased access to watch worldwide young elite dancers, the tricks are now being emulated without much, or any, concentration on the progressions or techniques behind these elements. That is why I have been approached to document and describe the processes that improve turns. During the research component of this book, I have interviewed 100 British teachers and dancers who have given me honest responses, highlighting their gaps of teaching knowledge with pirouettes. Their students admit that when it gets to the 'turns part' of the classes they don't really understand what they are doing, that the teaching of pirouettes is often rushed and rarely revisited.

I want to help. People often use the bumper sticker: *'Be the change you want to see in the world'*. Well, that is this book; it describes processes that I believe in and that I have seen results from. There are sections of this book for which my research took me to meet some of the most influential dance coaches and trainers in the world, and I am excited to share their opinions with you too. Dance is ever changing and we have to keep moving forward. There isn't just one way to improve but many. There are so many people to gain insight from.

Take this book as a vitamin C tablet to improve your understanding of pirouettes. You wouldn't cut out all other intakes of vitamin C; you'd just take it as a boost to what you already have.

FOREWORD:
AN INTERVIEW WITH SOPHIA LUCIA

A book on pirouettes would not be complete without any focus on the world record holder for multiple turns in passé position, the super talented 13-year-old, Sophia Lucia. I am so honoured that her name appears alongside mine in the title of this book; the little girl who changed the face of the world's turns.

World record holder Sophia Lucia with Rosina Andrews at Master Ballet Academy.

Never in my wildest dreams did I think that I would get the chance to meet Sophia, let alone see her dance or interview her personally. That dream came true when her agent, Deborah, at DBA Talent organised a meeting for me with her at her ballet school, Master Ballet Academy in Scottsdale, Arizona.

My experience at this school and with Sophia was so lovely; I really wanted to share it with my readers. The other amazing people I interviewed are separated in the chapter, 'Let's Talk Turns'.

My husband Sam (you will hear much more from him in this book; an ex-dancer too, who is now a qualified personal trainer and works closely training young dancers to use their bodies in a mechanically optimum way) and I arrived in the morning at Master Ballet Academy; the only globally recognised ballet school in the state of Arizona, lead by their master principal Slawomir Woźniak. A dancer of the Poznań Ballet, Slawomir made his professional debut at the Wroclaw Opera before going on to join the National Ballet of Warsaw as first soloist for many years. In 2000, Slawomir graduated from the Ballet Pedagogy at the Frederic Chopin Academy of Music in Warsaw. For many years he had conducted dance courses for young Americans during summer intensive programmes. It was a natural transition from being a principal dancer and an already recognised choreographer to become a teacher, and to be able to transfer his experience, knowledge and passion on to younger generations of ballet dancers. That is where Master Ballet Academy was born.

Reached through the desert and hills of sunny Arizona, Master Ballet Academy is unassuming, much to the contrary of the talent inside. On arrival we were greeted most warmly by Sophia's mum, Jaclyn, and her Grandma, as well as Slawomir and his assistant choreographer, Alberto. We were then introduced to Sophia, a charmingly polite young girl, who rushed off quickly into rehearsal. Straight away the atmosphere of the studio hit us as family-like; strict but fun. Young dancers were in the glass-doored studios being put through their paces, in privates, classes and rehearsals, yet all were smiling and happy, and their parents outside the rooms, the same, a rather rare occurrence a week before competition. We arrived the week before the YAGP finals, so the students were busily practising for this prestigious competition. We then spent a couple of hours watching rehearsals take place with some of the world's best known young ballet dancers, Juliet Doherty, Avery Gay, Brigid Walker, to name but a few. These students were at the top of their balletic game, with their teachers intricately honing their technique within complex and innovative balletic enchaînements. A sense of a new era of ballet exudes from the walls of this studio with students who are so versatile and advanced for their age.

The dancers entered and exited studios with grace and were so polite to everyone they met, saying 'good morning' and 'welcome' to the two random English people every time we crossed paths. They were immaculately groomed but all individual; not one student looked the same, something I am a massive advocate of. Uniform has its positives, but for me, a student who begins to trial leotards, skirts, shorts, etc. begins to have a personal identity, something that is so important in the dance world, not another clone, not someone who is following suit. There were a large number of young male dancers around, practising pas de deux, sky-high leaps and infinite turns, which was encouraging to see; as were the chocolate bars, juices and snacks that were being consumed in between classes!

Slawomir's aim for Master Ballet is to create the ballet principals of the future, to create a New York's Joffrey, Milan's La Scala, London's Royal Ballet, for dancers in the Midwest and West Coast. His aims are to develop dancers who can perform straight away for the company they have trained with. Oh so often he sees prestigious schools not even hire their own dancers in their companies, instead shipping them in from other establishments. He wants the best and freshest talent to take centre stage and with the Phoenix Ballet he is doing this. Some of his senior dancers were offered places with American Ballet Theatre; some took it, yet some remained with him. This highlights the great work he is doing and its popularity.

After a morning of watching rehearsals, it was time for our scheduled interview with Sophia. I had been made so at ease during the morning that the interview turned into an informal chat and I was so grateful for all Sophia had to say in answer to my questions.

Closing my eyes, it was hard to believe I was listening to a 13-year-old. In contrast to many 'Internet famous' children, she was incredibly humble, together and honest. Her understanding and explanation of her turns and technique was astounding and so intellectually delivered, her answers surpassed all of my expectations. This child is not just insanely talented, but impeccably intelligent too. She isn't just a naturally good dancer; she knows what she has to do and constantly works to develop it. As well as knowledgeable and 'real', Sophia is engaging and humorous, her anecdotes and jokes were great. This 13-year-old has so much natural confidence in an interview situation – her mum had gone out to the shops, so she sat there and held her own for the whole hour. At no point did I feel she was precocious or a diva, in fact the complete opposite, fame has come to her, she definitely hasn't gone searching for it. You will see from her interview below how genuine she is.

After the interview and some photos we had some candid time with her in the studio; it was amazing to chat to her about spray tans, where to go for lunch, her brother etc. Nothing was too much for this teenager and it wasn't manufactured, it was authentic. She even wanted a #plunginglunge in one of my merchandise T-shirts!

After a quick lunch (of course Sophia's recommendation), we were invited to the Master Ballet's showcase evening for their beneficiaries. A small, select and very important audience arrived, and it was surreal to be part of. We were only lucky enough to see the first few pieces, as our flight was that evening, but what a select few we saw. Also at the start of the performance, as MBA is very new, Slawomir described the school, its workings and how it hopes to progress worldwide, to then go on and mention me and my book to all these very important people was unreal.

Sophia definitely wasn't the only student in the studio that could turn, they all were perfectly on balance and connected to create the impressive rotations. The staff too, when demonstrating, were top-class. Watching Zherlin Ndudi demonstrate to a student, some 8/9 turns, can only highlight why the students are so good… the teachers are masters too. The student-teacher relationship was something to highlight too, so positive, so young and fresh. I am sure at times tensions run high, but happy students are impossible to fake.

I hope one day to return to this remarkable establishment, maybe send a few of my extension programme students to audition there, for what I saw was the future and with that a lot of passion. The dance world has to evolve and change and this studio embraces that.

Perfect pirouette positions with Sophia Lucia

Exclusive Interview with Sophia Lucia, April 2016

Can you remember when you first started turning?

Well it's always been in our repertoire and vocabulary of dance. I probably did my very first correct pirouette when I was about six. I learned how to turn when I was four.

Who was your first teacher?

The first teachers to teach me to pirouette were Lynn-Rae Hiers and Kristen Hibbs.

What can you remember from the first classes of turns that you did when you were six, what was focused on?

Our rules in our studio when I was little were very, very strict and however old you were was how many turns you did. And you got kicked out of class if that wasn't the total, you could still heel it* and it would count!
(*Heel it – put your heel down.)

Rachel Sebastian came into our studio when I was six years old and she was really about the positions of the turn, and we started working on a method called RAFT and that is my mentality for turns, and so I was able to master the RAFT by when I was nine.

So when you were ten, you could do ten turns?

My record in jazz shoes was about 22.

When you turn, RAFT is your method. What is that?

R – Rectangle – Which is different to most people when they turn, they think about a square, but if you teach kids this, they would get really short and not have a flat back.

A –Arch – Not just your highest relevé, the arch has to push over the second toe.

F – Focus – This is the most important I think. It helps me the most. A lot of people spot their head, but they don't see; they are glazed over. Basically with the glazed over look you can't find your balance, even if you're really strong and tight. If I was turning in a theatre, I try and find an exit sign or red dot. It's the specifics of what the eye can see. It has to be eye level or higher, never lower. When I do my fouettés on pointe I arch back, so I have to lean over a little more. Sometimes it helps if I look through the mirror into the clock.

T – Tightness – Not tension, as that can be misplaced, instead of in your core, you grip in your mouth or your hands. Kids do the one eyebrow; I tend to suck in my cheeks! I don't know why I do that.

That's the RAFT. That's the basics and that's how I break it down. There is more to turns than that though!

The preparation for turns is one of the most important steps to do wonderful turns. My version of turning is a lot different to normal people; my weight placement is a lot different. I have 95% in the front foot and 5% in the back, with jazz shoes. With pointe shoes, I have a little more weight in the back foot, just to feel a little more grounded.

I've noticed in your turns that your preparation is quite small…

Yes! The transfer of weight is super important; we used to spend hours and hours on the prep. You should have your highest arch at the back, not just on the turn but on the prep. That's why my back foot only has 5%, as if I didn't have my full arch then it would be more pressure.

What about speed and momentum?

We have the prep, the RAFT and then the speed and momentum. My favourite number to turn at would be an eight, which is quite fast! So, a lot of people tend to go too fast or too slow, so they have to feel where they are comfortable at. So that's the number I want to turn at, and so I have to set my speed. You have to make speed and momentum very, very good together, or else it's just spins. The momentum will take over and you're just spinning.

Such a science! I'm so glad you know what you're doing. You're so young to be so scientifically objective.

A lot of people think I can just turn, but I have really learnt how to do it and how to understand it, and I am one of Rachel's only students who have fully understood what she meant. I picked up on it so quickly.

How did you decide you wanted to be a world record holder and do you know what the record was before you broke it?

Yes I did, so it was actually quite funny. It came about because I couldn't hit ten pirouettes in my tap solo on stage, so my teacher said if I can do 20 in practice, ten will be no problem. So that's how it came about. Oddly enough, I was able to 20 straight away and she thought this was pretty unusual for an eight-year-old.

Twenty!

Yes, that was my consistent! *Giggles*
From there she was pushing me to get higher numbers because it was insane! I think that once we found out what the record was, which was 36, she was saying I think you could beat it! Twenty-six, twenty-seven was easy for me; we just needed to train on this. As soon as I went to 40, she was videotaping and that just went viral.

That set us off to try for the world record. There was a lot more expected of me than we thought however, we just thought we could do whatever positions and arms we wanted. If you notice, up until around 40, I was going passé to coupé then putting my arms up. Many dancers still say *I can do 36 pirouettes*, and I'm like *no, no, no! You changed positions!* So the rules of Guinness say you have to stay in one position the whole entire time. The actual official video I did 56 and then did not count the last one, because my passé foot disconnected! They videotaped in slow-mo, and then this annoying clicker, which put me off a bit!

I remember completely freaking out. Not many people know this, but I had about 400 people in the other room waiting to watch it. We had people drive from Seattle and Texas, so I was really nervous, as I only had three chances.

Which one did you end up going with?

That was the last chance! Technically I should be in the record book three times, as I broke it each time I did it! But I wasn't happy with what I was doing, I was really, really, REALLY frustrated. I remember it was on my very last try, I slipped before I did it, I stopped and said 'I thought we were practising!' and luckily he gave me another shot! I was almost in tears. When they started the video they had to start it from my feet because I was too upset! I remember we were laughing about that when we were cutting it for everyone.

So how many hours a week did you train to break that record?

I was dancing 45 hours a week, and then 20 of those were on turns. I remember I kept getting massages on my calves, as I was getting really hurt, and I also started breaking blood vessels in my hands because the centrifugal force was too much! If I tried it now I'd only be able to do 30 as my max. I mean if I trained I probably could, but my hands just can't handle it any more. I broke so many blood vessels, my hands can't handle it, they start to swell and then they get puffy, then they turn bright purple. They break out in hives and itch for two days. We try not to do it so much now.

Would you try and break a record again?

Well if I was able to, with my hands, I would.

Not sure if anyone will beat you though, you made the gap pretty big!

My ultimate record was 63. It doesn't count though, the adjudicator wasn't there!

We believe you, don't worry!
Do you find it easier to turn now you do more ballet?

No, I find it's much more difficult in turnout and pointe shoes. My turnout isn't the greatest. I've worked really hard this past 6 months training here on my turnout, but it's still not where it needs to be yet. For sure, I am able to do a lot more than I used to.

That video Master Ballet posted of you doing your variation was amazing!
(Sophia dances *Odalisque* with ten turns on pointe.)

I watch it back now and say, 'Slawomir, it's not even good!' Everyone is laughing, but it's not right. He says the quantity is fine, and I say,

'No, we're going for quality now! That's more important.' Everyone knows I can turn so it's about cleaning it up now rather than getting more! I've been offered to break the world record in pointe shoes and I don't want to. The most anyone has done on pointe is 16 and my record is 15. I'm close, I could if I wanted to, but my focus is somewhere else now. We're not going to pay to have that done.

Did you have to alter your technique through your growth spurt?

Nope. Everyone was freaking me out though, saying your turns won't be as good when you're older and things like that and they were dead serious. They were like, 'The way you turn just doesn't work for people.' I was like, 'OK.'

I went to Israel this past December to surprise this little girl for her Bat Mitzvah, me and my partner Jack, and basically she wanted a private on turns. This was the first time I taught someone who hadn't done turns like I had. She went from balancing and falling out of a single, to three consecutive turns. Gorgeous. It shows you that my method does work.

It's having the access to it too. Dancers start turning in the UK when they are around 12, which I always say is too late.

It is too late, I think too. I'm really blessed that I got flexible after I started turning. That is a big thing, if you look at rhythmic gymnasts, they probably weren't born that flexible. When I started doing rhythmics, I'd go and try and turn and just couldn't, because the back is so flexi. There's a couple of studios here in AZ who used to train a lot in flexibility and they just can't turn, because they don't have the right core and control. They don't have the same sense of it. When I have my own daughter, I'll do it the way I did it, turn then bend. Flexibility can always be improved.

Did rhythmic gymnastics help you?

It was definitely something that I needed. It opened a lot more capabilities of doing cool things that nobody else could. Our goal for the choreography of my solos was to be better than the last year and what can we do that no one else is doing. Sometimes you try and bring back the tricks and think, no, we did this when I was nine and now everyone does it! I don't think it helped my strength, if anything I got weaker, so I had to do a bunch of conditioning too.

So, Sam is a personal trainer and he does a lot of Pilates work with dancers.

No way! I'm jealous, we could have done Gyro!

Do you still do Pilates?

Yes I do, Gyrotonics and Pilates. I'm trying to convince my mum to take me to Hot Yoga but she won't let me, she says I'm not hydrated enough!

How much conditioning do you do a week?

I don't really count. Since I'm growing into a woman's body, we try and do as much cardio as possible, just because the ballerina image is very strict and I am absolutely not that at the moment. I try to do as much cardio and Gyrotonics, the Gyro is more for my turnout muscles. I've been able to find some more turnout after doing those classes. It still isn't as good as it needs to be, but I am working on it.

How do you stay up at the end of your turns?

I actually didn't know the answer to this until about seven months ago. Master Ballet opened a door when I came here. I like to watch the men turning and they have some of the best turners I have ever seen in my life here. They taught me how to stop with a turned out leg. You have your leg in your passé and then when you feel like momentum is speeding up you lift the passé. I've never been a fan of that, because it just shows you're not in your tightest position straight away. We talk about the four places you get momentum from: your supporting leg, your working leg, your arms and your spot. So, for me, I was really against changing how my turns worked. I was very strongheaded about it! I found that if you do it a certain way, different things work for different people. If I have my passé in its tightest position then I take a breath and it lifts a tiny bit, there's always more room to grow, it just stops me.

A lot of people use the analogy of opposition, there's always an opposition in dance if you think about it, for me that doesn't work. I've never thought of pressing the floor with my bottom foot, it just didn't work. In tap it might have because of the traction. In pointe shoes you're turning on two to three inches of a box and if you push down you're just going to hurt your toes! The dancer has to be smart enough to know their own body. I can teach it in detail, but if it's not working for the kid then it's not going to work. I was one of the lucky ones to do exactly what Miss Rachel was talking about! I found my own way of turning, not everything is her words, but I have a core of steel, if I am off balance I can save it. It doesn't look the prettiest but at least I can save it. Many people, because of how they are taught to turn, if they fall they are done. There's always turns when you fall. You want to know how to save it but that shouldn't be your goal.

When you turn do you think of your breathing?

I don't think so. Maybe that's why I have broken blood vessels! I try to do it now but do it the wrong way and end up falling.

Everyone has their own arm position for turns. What is your favourite?

A lot of people support the belly button thing, that doesn't work for me. You have to be as compact as possible so not to sink. I like to do it opposite my sternum bone and from that my pinky is in line. Elbows should be up too. Arms are a really big thing in turns; I could talk 45 minutes about arms! The prep of turns with the arms is very, very specific. If you are one inch wrong it isn't guaranteed. I've got my own way for arms, with pointe shoes I now mess it up a bit. It's higher and I have a lot further to fall. A lot of people I see videos of, there's a bunch of things they could improve on and I'm sure they're doing the same with me. I watched this video the other day, I wasn't even gasping over the girl, but this guy did eight inside turns! I love to watch people turn and watch people fail at turns too! I love to help people with turns, like my pas de deux partner never wants my advice for his turns! I have to put him in his place! He won't listen to RAFT because it's 'a jazz dancer's way'.

I love to watch men turn. The way they turn is how I want to turn, with more elegance. It's so smooth and breathless and they literally look like a spinning top.

My favourite routine is *Vienna*. What is your favourite from all those years?

Um, this is hard. The ones I love, people often say aren't their favourite. I have a connection with *Dream Catcher* and *Wishbone*. *Wishbone* I hated running, it felt so special on stage though. They were quite a challenge!

I think personally, the one that I got the most out of, just hearing the song and dancing to it gave me the chills, was probably *Secrets*. They're all by the same choreographer.

Who's your favourite choreographer?

Oh, sorry to everyone that I forget! I find it's really hard now to find choreography for me that hasn't been done or used before. I love Jason Parsons. I did his solo recently at YAGP, it's called *Come Undone*.

That's probably my favourite solo this year and everyone chuckles. My mum hated it, she thought I forgot how to dance because he wanted flexed feet and relaxed. I like him as he gave me a freedom with the story and every dancer needs a story. I was going through a really dark time when I learnt this solo, so it was really emotional. I connected with that one the most. I enjoy that one, it feels good.

I can tell you the people I want to work with!

Travis Wall is probably my number one! I've worked with Teddy Forance and he is amazing!

This might not be true… I read that you had one less rib! Does it help with turns or flexibility?

No! I was a premature baby, 3lbs and only have 11 ribs on each side, but it's not been an issue. I was never naturally good at anything. I wasn't meant to be a dancer. I was really bad for a long time, but I had a really good determination and Mum's always said nothing's come easy for me. I was never flexible until I went to rhythmic. In fact Mum stretches me every day for two hours. I'm not allowed to come to dance unless I'm stretched! I don't think the ribs were ever an issue. Everyone says that's why I'm so flexible, but no, if I was naturally flexible then yes, but I didn't have my splits until I was about seven! Turning was probably the only thing I was good at! Everything I've done has had to be 150% effort. I've had a lot of best friends who have natural talent but seen it go down the drain. Natural talent has to be based on desire and determination. Everyone always asks me what are the three words you'd describe yourself with? Probably humorous, determined and I can't remember the other one!

Humble?

Yeah, that's a good one! Thank you!

Were your parents dancers?

My mum was! My dad pretends he is a dancer!

What would you do if you couldn't dance?

Fashion! I love interior design. My mum was a make-up and hair artist so maybe that!

What are your opinions on young dancers' current trend to be hungry for fame?

I don't think that should be a goal.

I can tell by listening to you that isn't your goal at all.

I remember when I was really little Instagram was the thing and I wanted 10K so badly, and my brother was like 'What's your goal?' and I said 100K, but I don't know why! It's still weird for me. I'll go out to the movies and someone will ask for a photo, and I'm like, 'Wait. What!' Random things… If I'm out with my dad shopping, I don't get to see him very often, we're still not used to it. I never really thought that would be me, I thought maybe it would be when I'm older. Now I'm older I take responsibility more and don't let people use me so much. I remember at dance competitions I used to be so nervous I'd just say yes to everyone and was always unprepared. I'm really stubborn about having my time and personal space, but I had to earn it. I don't mean to be short or abrupt, but I'm like 'Sorry I'm warming up. Come to me after I finish dancing'.

The very first moment I realised my followers were gaining, I didn't think it was real, I thought my brother had bought the followers, and he said, 'Didn't you just do a TV show?' And I was like yes, I'd just done *Shake it Up* and I'd been in the commercial dancer world so done some commercials and TV shows here and there. But it's like a 'pinch me' moment and it's still the same now.

I remember at the competition, Showstoppers, and my *Dance Moms* episode had just aired (I am very thankful for that, and they showed me in a good light); there were three rooms, the biggest comp of the USA. I remember I was so nervous because I couldn't get from my dressing room to the stage, all three rooms stopped to watch and I was 20 minutes late on because I was swarmed. So I was freaking out. I didn't know how to handle it. I didn't know what was going on. It was chaotic. I had to bring my own tent to change in because kids were going underneath bathroom stalls to get pictures. They were trying to get photos when I was getting undressed. That's why I need personal space. Primarily I want to be my best self. I don't want to be famous. It's not even on the list of things I want. I'm amazed people want to get to know me and get to know my story. People don't see that I was personally trained on Instagram when they try and copy. I think kids should find the right teachers to train properly, the kid that could be great ends up getting injured.

If you want to be a good dancer, you have to be humble and true to yourself. I was doing a TV show a couple of weeks ago and they wanted me to be someone that I was not. And I've grown up too, so people say, 'Where has the sweet, squeaky little girl gone?'!

What made you transition into ballet?

This is an interesting story, not many people know this. I was not happy with dance last year, I was at breaking point of quitting and I don't know if I was burnt out or if there wasn't a challenge any more. I got hired to do the spring show for Masters and I absolutely fell in love with Slawomir and felt like it was time. I'd outgrown my dance teachers and had no one at my dance studio to look up to. I was so tired of doing the same thing and my motto is always find something that challenges you. I didn't like how I was dancing or how I was feeling. I lost my spark. I came here last May and refound it. I came here and I said 'Mom, what am I missing?' and she said 'Ballet'. I had to sit down with my parents and ask if I could move to Arizona, as financially it would be very difficult, as I'm not on a scholarship here. I have a brother at home too. So luckily my grandma was able to move out with us and I have been loving it ever since.

I didn't know what I wanted to do with my life, there's no contemporary company I want to be in except Shaping Sound and by the time I'm old enough they might not still be around. So I didn't know. I was really lost so I started doing acting and booked some pilots that is when I came here and found myself. The goal was to do YAGP and I have the finals next week. I also wanted a challenge. I've danced with boys before but not in this way and me and Jack, you saw us, we bicker like brother and sister. I found a new challenge in pas de deux, not just the ballet, which is so humbling. I have a new appreciation of what men do. Pas de deux is really difficult on stamina, mentally and physically. I just got back from eight days' break and we're still trying to get our timing back together.

Is that your long-term goal, a ballet company?

Yes. If I don't make it classically, perhaps Nederlands Dans Theater or something like that. I want to be in the UK or Europe where ballet is worshipped. You don't go to the movies, you go to the ballet.

After I can't dance, I want to act, but if I can't do that I will teach. I want to be a movie drama actress, like Jennifer Lawrence!

And do you use a TurnBoard?

Gosh no, I hate them!

Kids Instagram Questions!

I posted on my social media that I would ask Sophia any questions from my fans. She agreed, of course, and the answers are below!

What's your favourite dancewear brand? – Cali Kisses.

Favourite dance style? – Ballet or contemporary.

When did you start? – Two years old.

Goals? – Ballet companies.

Do you feel like giving up? – Yes I feel like everyone does, you have to find your spark.

How many hours a day do you train? – Eight to ten hours.

***Tap Diva* was amazing. How old were you and do you still tap?** – Yes I still do, I was 10.

How many pirouettes in bare feet? – Oh, I have no calluses on my feet because they hurt in the pointe shoes, so something like five. That's really dumb!

What's your motivation to stretch? – I don't have motivation. I can't go to dance if I don't.

How many turns when you were three? – Maybe one or two.

Are you homeschooled and do you regret it? – I have absolutely no regrets; I've been homeschooled since third grade. It's a lot of work and you have to be really focused, and I am sociable as it has a stigma that we're not. I have a teacher as I have to stay on top of it. And if not my parents would have to do it and I'm a Daddy's girl so I'd probably get an A even if I deserved a D.

1. THE SCIENCE OF TURNING

Whilst I promised that this book wouldn't be full of scientific formulas and humourless physics, a book on turning couldn't be without just a smidgen of theory and my inner grammar school geek secretly loved writing this chapter! I won't be offended if you choose to skip it or just skim the pages looking at the pretty pictures! Let's get the boring bit out of the way first!

Over the past 50 years, dance science, as well as research into the biomechanics of movement, has advanced tremendously along with dancers' and dance teachers' interest in the subject. Nowadays, studying an MSc in dance science at Trinity Laban Conservatoire, London, is quite a common post-professional dance career prospect. No longer is dancing enough; people want to know how we move and are always searching for the optimum prerequisites and exercises to create the 'best dancer'. It is sad, as often the artistry is forgotten and we feel like we are creating robots by basing our practice on the results of experiments using tools and graphs, eradicating anomalies and discovering consistent practices within movement. We must remember that we should be using science to enhance our dancers' bodies and optimise their movement, without losing the natural creativity and freedom that sets good dancers apart from amazing dancers. We are obligated to try and connect art with science and not detach them; easier said than done.

Biomechanics is the study of the structure and function of biological systems by the methods of 'mechanics' – which is the branch of physics involving analysis of the actions of forces. Biomechanics in sports can be described as: the muscular, joint and skeletal actions of the body during the execution of a given task or skill. Proper understanding of biomechanics relating to a sports skill has the greatest implication on: sporting performance, rehabilitation and injury prevention, along with sport mastery.

Biomechanics within dance helps us gather information to analyse motion, understand muscle use and locate where forces act upon the body. These then help us with teaching methods, skill development and injury prevention. Scientists focus on each part of the body and then use these for investigation within dance movements. Kinematic (the geometry of movement) processes are all observed in the biomechanics of dance, helping describe the motion: how far, how fast etc. and then allowing the research to notice important events in the performance of the skill. Alongside this, kinetic processes highlight the 'cause and effect' association within movement. This part of the research involves the forces (torques) acting within the body, e.g. how bones, muscles and connective tissue collaborate to ascertain the amount of muscle use required to create the desired movement. Kinetics focuses on internal processes and then moves on to those processes that affect force from the external environment. The improvement of dance shoes and dance floors has been greatly advanced by kinetic research over the past few years.

There are many tools and machines used by scientists to understand the forces acting upon the body, and most importantly for my research, into turns, generating further information about the movement of centre of mass and gravity. Biomechanics has been said to *close the gap between the reality of movement and our understanding of it*. Y. Kwon, who is an advocate of including mechanical perspectives in dance training, addresses issues of safety and mechanics at the same time as honouring dance as an art.[1]

There are hundreds of research articles on the biomechanics of dance movements, but I have just selected to review the research processes of those for passé (as the Americans call it colloquially, or 'retiré' for us British*), then leading on to research of the movement analysis of pirouettes and touching upon research findings regarding balance optimisation. There are many other factors within the process of

1   Kwon, Y. *Study of dance in the mechanical perspective: dance biomechanics. Korean J Dance. 2001,9:124-30*

pirouetting that have been subject to vast research too, including placement of arms, alignment of pelvis, use of plié and ability to spot.

The official difference between passe and retire is that passe is the actual movement in which the leg passes the knee of the supporting leg from one position to another and retire is the position itself.

Scientifically, there are three key characteristics that affect the execution of the movement; body form, balance and the speed of the turns. The positioning and movement of a turn will be discussed throughout this book, but now I will share further knowledge associated with the biomechanics of the movement helping generate further knowledge and understanding of the movement itself. With a biomechanical mindset, the important parts of a pirouette are not the positioning of the arms, or the specific spotting action. Instead a scientist's focus is upon the distribution of body weight around the central axis, the way in which the torque is exerted to start the angular momentum of the turn, and where the dancer's centre of gravity (COG) is. A skilled dancer should be able to keep their turning axis vertical, therefore their COG stays constant.

Centre of Gravity (COG) – A Little Bit of Science

A person's COG plays an important part in their balance. When standing, the COG is in the abdomen. In preparation for a turn the COG shifts slightly back into the lower back and then as the turn begins it shifts to the front of the body.

Dancers are often taught to perform pirouettes by starting the movement in balance and then keeping the body rigid in that configuration, as opposed to correcting any imbalance.

An experiment focusing on this is described in the *Journal of Dance Medicine & Science*,[2] and I think it highlights some important factors for dancers.

---

2   Lott, Melanie B., Laws, Kenneth L. The Physics of Toppling and Regaining Balance during a Pirouette. (2012) *Journal of Dance Medicine & Science*, 16(4), p.167.

The research calculated the angle at which nine advanced dancers lost stability in a turn and had to hop on their supporting leg. It was recorded that the hop happened when the angle displaced $9.3 \pm 1.9°$ from vertical. This highlights that a near perfect balance is required to perform multiple turns without any realignment.

The results demonstrate that holding the body rigid makes it difficult to achieve consistent rotations, whereas dancers would have more consistency if they were taught strategies for regaining balance.

There are three ways in which dancers can regain balance:

1. Returning the COG to a location on top of the supporting foot (SF). This can be done by altering the alignment of the upper body, moving the arms down or shifting the pelvis forward.
2. Hopping the SF to a place directly below the COG.
3. Sliding the SF to a place directly below the COG.

Whilst we do not want our dancers to form a habit of hopping or changing position, we do want them to understand the processes and be able to make decisions within their mechanical actions to save turns if they need to. This is where training dancers with a dynamic turning posture is always advantageous.

Quick Biomechanical Glossary

Motion	Motion with Spin	Dance Teacher Lingo...
Velocity	Angular Velocity	How fast we turn. It is identical to the rate of spin. It refers to the rotations done in a given time frame.
Mass	Rotational inertia	Shaping of position of arms and legs. The body's resistance to rotational motion increases when more mass is distributed further from the axis of rotation.

Motion	Motion with Spin	Dance Teacher Lingo...
Momentum	Angular momentum	The repeated turn. A multiple turn.
Force	Torque	The push off the floor, the use of the abdominals and placement of arms used to create movement power when we prepare.

If we describe a simple single pirouette, it is a 360 degree rotation of the body on one foot.

- The angular velocity describes the speed of the pirouette yet also its magnitude. (Quantity.)
- Rotational inertia is affected by the change of the dancer's position during a pirouette, for example using your arms to speed you up, or losing the arm positioning to alter the success of balance in your retiré position.
- Angular momentum makes an appearance when the pirouette changes from non-repetitive (a single pirouette) to a repetitive movement (multiple pirouettes).

It is important to understand that angular momentum refers to a vector quantity that represents the product of a body's rotational inertia and rotational velocity about a particular axis. According to the parallel axis theorem, a pirouette is referred to as a "remote" term where the moment of inertia of a body is rotating about its external pivot and is equal to the product of mass and distance squared. (Blazevich, A. J. 2012).

Angular momentum = Angular velocity x Rotational inertia

Pirouette Surgery® Survey Results

A hundred dancers from throughout the UK were interviewed. These are dancers who are not taught by me on a regular basis.

How old are you?

The average age of the participants was 14 years.

Do you like pirouettes?

39% answered NO, 61% answered YES.

If you answered no, why not?

The responses to this question fell into the categories below:

- *Become dizzy*
- *Afraid of them*
- *Lose control*
- *Never learnt them*
- *Can't balance*
- *Intimidation*
- *Inconsistent*

Can you remember the first time that you tried a pirouette? How old were you?

The average age was 11 years. It ranged from 8 years to 18 years.

Think back to the first time you did a pirouette. Did your teacher:

- **Spend a lot of time teaching the process of the pirouette?**
  37% answered YES, 63% answered NO.
- **Teach a range of exercises before the actual pirouette?**
  41% answered YES, 59% answered NO.
- **Revisit the technique of a pirouette regularly since then?**
  45% answered YES, 55% answered NO.

When you execute pirouettes what things often go wrong?

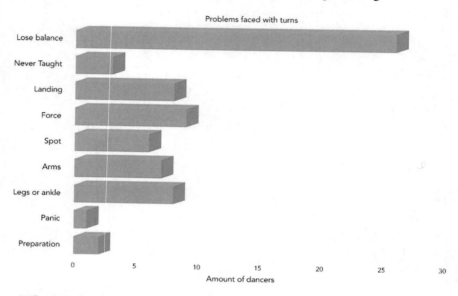

What is the maximum number of turns you can do with the correct technique?

The average was 1.9.

Amount of turns

 Single
 Double
■ Triple
■ Quadruple

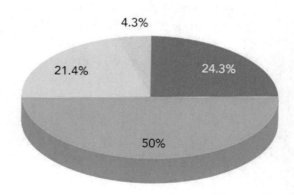

Completed after the Pirouette Surgery® class

Do you feel like your pirouettes have improved since the technique focus class?

100% said YES!

Which pirouette drill in the class did you find the most beneficial?

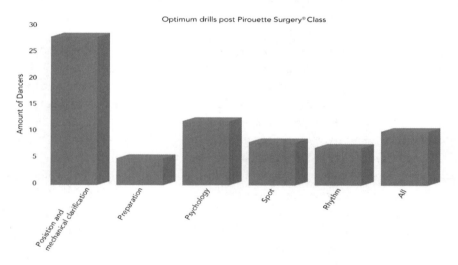

Evaluation

Without breaking these results down and psychoanalysing them all to deeply, I think it is clear to see that turns would be better for all dancers if they were able to have clearer training and access to them. The average age to start turns and the number of turns executed, in comparison to those talked about by Sophia and Autumn from the USA, highlight a rather large difference in training here in the UK. Whilst we cannot change everything, I hope that this book will start to get these numbers and the turning enthusiasm, up slightly.

Many people think that the inclusion of lots of turns in dance is a new thing. We only have to observe the iconic ballets to see a lot of turns, but the turns seem to be apparent more and more, especially in online videos. With a family in dance, I have had lots of conversations with elders about the past industry of dance and it seems things like acrobatics, turning and intricate leaps are nothing new, just something that is now more apparent in the dance world. The Internet has had a massive impact on how dance is now observed and inspiration is now all over our daily lives. I love the little anecdote below about multiple turns from the past...

In Los Angeles, I have my Hollywood Grandma, we are not related but she is just like a Grandma to my husband and I every time we visit. Joy Hewitt is a tap legend in the USA, she just throws into conversation that she taught Patrick Swayze to tap dance and has a whole list of celebrity dance friends. The real icons in our industry! Well, to cut a long story short, she lives with another legend, Jim Taylor. He was Ginger Rogers' partner on her comeback tour. He's worked with everyone, he's choreographed everywhere and he knows everything dance related. One evening, like wide-eyed toddlers, we sat and listened to all of their thespian and theatrical stories and the topic of turns came about. Jim shared the below with me, and it highlights that multiple turns are nothing new and can steal you the job!

Jim Taylor

'In the seventies I auditioned for Michael Kidd, the original choreographer for Seven Brides for Seven Brothers, Guys and Dolls *etc. The movie he wanted dancers for was* Star!. *It was based on the life of Gertrude Lawrence, starring Daniel Massey and Julie Andrews. We got called up and he said, 'OK, let's see everyone do quadruple pirouettes'. They then went down the line. I was at the wrong end of the line and watched a lot of good turns before me, but I was lucky I pulled off those four pirouettes and got the job. That movie had 12 production numbers over 4 hours... it was a complete flop.'*

PIROUETTE – a quick, biomechanical and dance science review of the movement this whole book is based on.

Let's think of the pirouette as a science experiment... the objective: to complete as many rotations as possible with an aesthetic dance position.

Please note all of the parts of the turn are described in further depth in their personal chapters. This is about the biomechanical processes that are used to turn.

We hope 'the results' will be consistent, yet we are likely to find anomalies when our technique isn't perfect.

Perfect pirouettes as a dance skill are particularly challenging, they need constant repetition and technical control of the body. The dancers also need to have a good sense of turning and lack fear. Starting to turn at a young age can help conquer any fear, as long as the experiences are positive.

Phase 1 – Preparation

There are very few biomechanical principles here as there is no movement. The optimum starting position uses good posture with an engaged core, creating good pelvic and spinal alignment. See 'The Goldilocks Complex'.

Phase 2 – Creating the Torque

The primary biomechanical principles in this position include the stabilisation of the arms and a deep plié: a moving and lengthening plié as opposed to a stagnant bend. The dancer's centre of gravity is low in this position, therefore the topple factor is very low and falling from this position is very unlikely. Unless you've had a couple of beers!

Initial Torque

What is this word 'torque'? Torque is a force; in a pirouette it is the preparation and push. We all assume that the only torque in a pirouette is the foot pushing off the floor – this is of major importance and the only torque in smaller number pirouettes, however, there is also torque produced in the body for the larger number pirouettes. Once a dancer is on relevé, no additional force can be put into the body as a turning system. The preparation position itself is of main importance. If you are not aligned correctly in the plié you may have erased any chance of performing successful turns. That being said, there are many dancers whose balletic placement at the barre, and even in the centre, do not comply with 'good alignment' observations, but when it comes to turning, they snap into a correct alignment!

Stabilization of the Trunk

During the push off into the pirouette it is imperative to not allow flexion in the trunk. We never want to see retraction of the ribcage to alter the alignment and aim to use protraction in our abdominal practice to help stabilise the movement. Using the latissimus dorsi and deltoids, force can be created with horizontal adduction to move the side arm into our en avant position, which involves shoulder flexion. Our deep transverse abdominals, with our posterior muscles of the back, will keep the trunk upright.

Biomechanical Errors in Preparation

Leg Pronation – where the ankle, foot and calf do not align.
I often see this happen when dancers think that they will get more push off their whole foot as opposed to their toes. I relate this to riding a scooter, you can't get much push off just your big toe joint!

Biomechanical Errors at the Start of the Turn

- Rotating in the wrong direction… Doh!
- Arms open past 180 degree and flung behind the shoulder.
- The concentric contraction at the knee joint is inadequate, so less push can be used.
- Arm contractions are derisory; arms are, therefore, not rounded.
- Plantar flexion lacking.

Phase 3 – Turn

There is also a misconception on what position 'good turners' turn in. When asked to demonstrate the position in which they turned without the turn, they demonstrate the desired and documented aesthetically pleasing position. If, however, we observed their position whilst turning, the body wisdom has overridden the aesthetics and placed the arms, and sometimes the legs, into a more mechanically efficient one. That or one that highlights to us all why the turn is going completely wrong!

We all strive for perfection with our dancers but we must remember that, dare I say it, even some of the best dancers cheat to make things even more impressive. I always say to my dancers, single up to quad turns must be done in a perfect pirouette position, using all the principles laid out in this book. After four turns, greater numbers of rotations need to be personalised and dancers must find positions that work for them. That being said, I don't expect the position to change drastically. Examples of minuscule alteration include: the arms lowering or closing to aid the centre of gravity; the foot to slightly cross the leg in a balletic turn; the preparation to have different syncopation; and to come from a smaller size fourth.

'So Rosina, you are telling me that to get my dancers to do more turns they need to cheat? I'd like a refund please!'

Hear me out; I'll change your opinion, I promise! Plus I've researched some rather big names and highlighted their 'modifications'. (Hey, that sounds better than cheats!)

To add this to your classes be careful not to introduce the concept of modifying too young. Train them to turn perfectly until they're around 13/14 years, when they have the concept of the perfect turn, before beginning to give them any option of change! The reason I advocate caution is that junior dancers are very mouldable and their muscle memories are very ripe and absorbing. In the long run, double or triple pirouettes need to be performed with confidence at auditions with perfect technique and if you allow your little ones the chance to mould the turn to suit them, the perfect turn will get very blurred too! Plus the modifications are tiny and unnoticeable for the untrained, and sometimes trained, eyes, and the concept of doing anything subtly is often lost with young dancers!

Here's an example of a professional who has altered their position into a mechanically optimum position.

Mikhail Baryshnikov

DanceSanity's Nathan Prevost has taken an in-depth look into Mikhail Baryshnikov's turns in the movie *White Knights*, where he demonstrates eleven pirouettes.[3]

Right at the very start in the preparation, the closing arm is right behind him, although he hasn't changed his shoulders at all, they are still right over his hips. He builds momentum with this twist in the arms.

He then winds up into the turn. His passé position is crossed at the knee. Nathan Prevost states that: 'if he did that position at the barre his teacher would smack him with a stick'*. His arms also take a while to hit the 'proper ballet' position. They finally close, from a gradual closing movement, into en avant after his sixth turn. After seven turns they begin to lower. At the eleventh turn, to finish and come out of the turns, he extends his arms back up and out. Scientifically this creates greater inertia, slowing the turn down and stabilising it, allowing him to soften and lift at the end of the pirouettes. Prevost states that he has used this technique for many years, whether it be in single or multiple turns.

Wouldn't we all!

Evaluating his crossed passé position, firstly we must mention that he

---

3   Prevost, N. (2016). *The Sound of a Pirouette and Tips on Mastering Multiples*. [online] Danceadvantage.net. Available at: http://www.danceadvantage.net/multiple-Pirouettes/ [Accessed 24 May 2016].

is wearing street shoes, such as an Oxford dance shoe, as opposed to ballet shoes. He is also wearing trousers, so this will have affected the height of the passé due to the movement in the fabric. However, he is so high up on his demi-pointe position, which I will mention often in this book. The high, locked out demi-pointe position and strong ankle, creates a straight line down the back of the body as well as engaged glutes and optimal pelvis position.

The head is the densest part of the body, and if we were turning on glass or ice, just the movement of the head would enable a spinning action. Baryshnikov demonstrates a strong spotting action, which actually gets more brutal towards the final few turns. This being said, it is very easy to allow a strong head movement to throw the rest of the body out of alignment. Baryshnikov does not allow this to happen, I would assume because the strength in the movement of the heaviest part of his body correlates to the extreme strength in his core.

Prevost states that Sophia Lucia does not move her arms with her large numbers of multiple pirouettes, they stay in a very rounded, high en avant position, higher than an average position, opposite her sternum. He states that it is not 100% necessary to graduate the arms into the position, although it does aid some people. Sophia talks about her arm positioning in her interview.

My favourite quote of Nathan's during his evaluation of these turns is: 'I don't care if you do 72 pirouettes, if you fall out of it, the audience doesn't care'. (One of my students got that exact statement on a competition report: 'It doesn't count if you do five turns on your heel'… Well let's be honest guys, it doesn't!)

In evaluation, Baryshnikov alters his foot placement and the length of time it takes for his arms to hit the final position, to make his turns mechanically optimum for his body type and consistent in performances. (The complete video and study of this can be found on the Dance Advantage blog, www.danceadvantage.net/multiple-Pirouettes/)

The Science of Balancing During Pirouettes

What is balance? Is it strength? Is it focus? It's probably both.

Firstly let's concentrate on the brain's processing of focus.

How many times do we act like we are focusing on one thing when secretly were also thinking of something else? Uncommitted to either thought, the success of either is rather low. The brain can process one thought properly. Being able to multitask is a myth. Whilst being able to physically move different parts of our bodies at the same time, our brain's attentional capacity is not capable of more than one activation. So, it is no wonder that our students can't balance when their focus is everywhere but their balance! Once the position is ingrained in their muscle memory then their focus should purely be on balancing. If they look at themselves in their eyes in the mirror and concentrate only on the one task needed, to balance, then their balance will improve.

No, just picking someone off the street and training them to think that they're turning isn't going to turn them into a contender to beat Sophia Lucia's record, but training your dancers' minds in order to separate their thoughts and use the one that is needed, alongside the hours of conditioning, practice and performance, will definitely add a further element to their consistency.

Let's now focus on the dancer's position helping their balance.

You can't turn if you can't balance in the correct position. Again, as I said, if you are not here for the science, skip ahead, I won't be offended!

In a pirouette the body needs to be balanced, or in equilibrium, when a vertical line is drawn from the centre of mass (CM) and falls within the boundaries of the area of the support at the floor (in our case the base of support is the ball of the foot in demi-pointe on the supporting leg) (Lott and Laws, 2012). An object's CM is the point at the centre of its weight distribution, where the force of gravity can be considered to act on the body as a whole (Laws, 2008). Dancers are often taught to perform successful pirouettes by beginning the movement in balance and then keeping the body as stiff as possible in that position, contrasting to correcting for an imbalance with small adjustments during the turn. However, this is not a completely correct, optimum position for the dancer, as discussed further in the 'Sellotape Phenomenon'. Learning dancers should keep their bodies strong but slightly relaxed while holding a dynamic pose. If a dancer makes their body too rigid, the slightest displacement from perfect balance will cause gravity to add a force on the body, inevitably leading the dancer to topple and fall out of the pirouette. However, if the dancer allows for some movement, their body is able to make the slight adjustments necessary to correct itself during the turn and regain balance. We often see this when dancers hop, or move their arms.

Scientists, Lott and Laws,[4] state that there are two mechanisms to save a pirouette after imbalance. Firstly, moving the centre of mass, the dancer's body, back over the supporting foot, and secondly, moving the supporting foot back underneath the centre of mass. Whilst aesthetically we do not want our dancers to hop, it does show knowledge of their bodies and also the ability to save a turn if it goes wrong; something only advanced and body-aware dancers will be able to do.

Results from the study show that if a dancer begins the pirouette between 0.1 and 1 degrees off the perfect vertical plane, with centre of mass over the supporting foot, their chances of executing multiple turns is higher. Now the likelihood of dancers being able to consistently hit perfect alignment, or if they don't hit perfect alignment, have the ability to alter the body's balance to successfully save the turn, can only become habit by doing one thing, repetition.

During the turn you are losing energy due to friction. If you want to produce more than triple pirouettes you will need to convert some

4   Lott, M. B., Laws, K. L. (2012). *The Physics of Toppling and Regaining Balance During a Pirouette*. Journal of Dance Medicine & Science, 16 (4), 167-174.

energy (moment of inertia) stored in your arms and even the passé leg, into rotational force (angular momentum). Ice skaters show this conversion in a very impressive and simple to understand way. Suddenly during a calm, extended spin, the skater pulls their arms and legs nearer the axes and spins much faster. Arms are the biggest contributing factor to changing the speed of turns and this is explored further in the section 'A *T. Rex* Can't Turn'.

Phase 4 – The Finish

Most teachers and professional dancers say the ending is more important than the turn, but where a pirouette ends is up for discussion! For me, a pirouette finishes up, then the dancer chooses where to move on to, whether it be: in a lunge (or perhaps a #PlungingLunge); a step forward or to the side; an extension; a leap; anything. Luckily not much choreography that includes turns requests the dancer to remain in passé position for a few seconds before moving on to the next move, but unfortunately for dancers this sometimes creates obstacles in completing more turns, as habit has ingrained the choreography on the end of the pirouettes into muscle memory. In my Three Level Turning Programme I have developed a lot of exercises that help with maintaining the balance upwards at the end of a turn and not falling out of it, therefore allowing control over the next movement and also that extremely impressive ending. Being able to stop, up on demi-pointe, after five turns, is something only dreams, or YourDanceChannel on YouTube, are made of... or is it? (My dancers can do this!) Both Sophia Lucia and Autumn Miller talked to me about this process.

Scientifically, something that is spinning from an initial force will stop eventually, due to forces created by the surface it is rotating on, force in the air and a few other deeply scientific forces, which we can just skip over! Newton's first law states that an 'object at rest will stay at rest and an object in motion will stay in motion at the same velocity until it is acted on by an external force'. Therefore, if a dancer is pirouetting in a position that is perfectly balanced they should gradually slow down to stop in the same position that they were turning in.

Many dancers like to open their arms to finish a turn and to stabilise, similar to a parachute opening. How many turns you have done and how stable your torso is when your arms make the movement will determine the success of this action, however it is one that I highly recommend especially with balletic turns. Other dancers prefer to keep their arms in a tight en avant position, and completely lock into their shoulder positioning to create that stopping motion. I like to use the imagery of putting their brakes on at the end of the turn by adding further push and force into the floor through the supporting demi-pointe. This also engages the glutes and hamstring area, which has often been engaged at the start of the turn but by the end of it may have relaxed off slightly.

Notable Scientific Studies into Passé position and Pirouettes[5]

In 1998, the first study[6] into this movement involved a two-camera motion analysis system using dancers performing passé movements in different conditions. Results showed that trunk movement and stabilisation precedes limb activity.

This means stability in the core is paramount and majorly effects the position.

In reference to training, this highlights the importance of core strengthening exercises and also that a solid torso will aid the turns.

In 2003 Sandow, Bronner, Spriggs, Bassile and Rao,[7] compared expert dancers to beginners, executing passé position from a two-legged preparation position. One thing that this research suggested was that the elite dancer was able to maintain postural control prior to the movement, which aided their balance; this wasn't seen with the beginners.

---

5   Krasnow, D., MS, M. Wilmerding, V. PhD, Stecyk, S. PhD, ATC, CSCS, Wyon, M. PhD, and Koutedakis, Y. PhD, 2011. Biomechanical Research in Dance: A Literature Review

6   Bronner, S., Brownstein, B. A kinematic analysis of the passé in skilled dancers [abstract]. Journal of Dance Medicine & Science 1998;2(4)149.

7   Sandow, E., Bronner, S., Spriggs, J., Bassile, C. C., Rao, A. K. A kinematic comparison of a dance movement in expert dancers and novices [abstract]. Journal of Orthopaedic & Sports Physical Therapy 2003;33(2):A-25.

Focusing purely on the preparation, this study shows the massive importance of a solid and correctly aligned preparation position. When touring the country the preparation positions are what I find need the most focus and readjustment.

In 1972 an early thesis by McMillan[8] noted in Laws' research, compared the execution of pirouettes from three levels of dancers; professionals, dance major students and beginners, observing their preparations, turns and conclusions. Results showed that of the three phases; the preparation had the most similarities amongst the three groups. However, the professional dancers took much less time in the preparation phase. The skilled dancers showed a difference in spotting technique, arm positions, foot placement and acceleration.

In 1978, Laws and colleagues conducted several studies on turns.[9] Observing a professional ballet dancer over 50 trials, demonstrating pirouette en dehors, arabesque turns and pirouette en dedans, Laws described the turns qualitatively and suggested ways of turning with better technique and efficiency.

Continuing his research, Laws joined Fulkerson[10] in 1992/93 and investigated pirouettes in a more modern way by collecting data by video. Using formulas they concluded that 'the number of turns was dependent on the initial momentum and balance limited the number of turns possible'.

Dancers and dance teachers today must reference this; there are limiting factors, which mean that pirouettes cannot be infinite when demonstrated by a human.

---

8   Laws, K. L. An analysis of turns. Dance Research Journal 1978–79;11/1–2:12–19.

9   Laws, K. L. An analysis of turns. Dance Research Journal 1978–79;11/1–2:12–19.

10   Laws, K., Fulkerson, L. The slowing of pirouettes. Kinesiology and Medicine for Dance 1992/1993;15(1 Fall/Win):72–80.

In 1992 Meglin and Woollacott[11] used neuroscience research to create a theoretical model for turns. This research never became an article, however the main focus of the research summarised some really important ideas:

1. Posture anticipates gesture *(therefore alignment is more important than the action that creates the turn).*
2. Peripheral inputs allow immediate corrections *(summarising that dancers have the ability to alter the outcomes of their turns).*
3. The final position is processed in advance.
4. Differing areas of the brain are involved in the execution of turns.

Physics in the Fouetté

Again the dancer starts turning by creating a force, torque, in the preparation off the floor. The trickier part is maintaining the rotations because as the dancer turns friction from the floor, and also some from the air, slows them down. In a fouetté action further torque is created by the foot lowering from demi-pointe and the ball of the foot pushing against the floor. The arms are used to aid balance. The bending and straightening of the leg allows, by its continuous motion, the storing of momentum which is then transferred back to the dancer's body. Within fouettés the movement of the leg helps move momentum forward and back between leg and body and keeps them in motion.

The longer the leg is extended the more momentum it stores so therefore more turns can be produced before needing to replenish the force that's lost by friction. Again, bringing the arms and legs in closer to the body, decreasing the moment of inertia, will allow the dancer's turns to increase in speed.

---

11   Meglin, J. A., Woollacott, M. The neural choreography underlying a Pirouette arabesque. Kinesiology and Medicine for Dance 1992;14:95–105.

Can You Be a Natural Turner?

With the right training and skills I believe everyone can turn. At the end of a Pirouette Surgery® workshop, every attendant gets the chance to show me what they've got and I assign them all a unique correction and things to work on relating solely to them. It frustrates me massively if I cannot help. However, whether the correction springs to mind in 10 seconds or if it takes 10 minutes, I have been able to find one thing for everyone to improve… well I have done so far! I even found myself doing this when I visited Master Ballet Academy… It was good to know that the corrections I was thinking were the same as those voiced by their teachers!

Therefore, I do not agree when people say, 'Oh I'm not a natural turner!' They really mean that they don't like turning and everyone is allowed preferences in our free world. Nevertheless, some people find turning much simpler than others. Sometimes these are newer dancers who haven't yet developed the stress or lost their 'Wheeeeeeeeee Factor'. Sometimes it is dependent on the dancer's personality, whether they are brave and willing to take risks, and sometimes it is dependent on their body shape. I would never say that it is reliant on their training exclusively. Some dancers have trained at fantastic schools and spent lots of time and focus on turns, but they still don't like them!

Teachers and choreographers often have different expectations for large and small dancers, those that are more curvy and those who are more streamlined, but there are physical analyses that can help us understand these physique factors on certain types of movement, especially those involved with horizontal accelerations and pirouettes.

The taller dancer can exert more force because their muscles have a larger cross-sectional area than the shorter dancer, however because their body shape produces a larger rotational inertia, the speed of the turn is likely to be slower. The difference in size of preparation will affect the force installed into the turn, however this needs to be particularly high to equal the rotational acceleration of the smaller dancer.

From the view of physics, an optimum body for turning isn't one that we associate with dancers. Similar to a spinning top it would need a large centre, shorter and stubby legs, long toes of equal length and a tiny head. Hardly the requirements for most 'ballet school' auditions!

In evaluation, it seems that smaller, more compact dancers find turns easier, because their muscle mass is spread over short arms and their centres of gravity are lower and wider than taller dancers. Contrastingly, taller dancers are defying the laws of physics by training their bodies to turn in mechanically efficient ways, sometimes bypassing the perfect aesthetic listed as requirements on paper. Aligning their centre of gravity in a way that works for their body type and often the biggest factor that must change is the arm alignment. There is further reference to this in 'A T. Rex Can't Turn' and also in the interview with Krista Miller.

Spinning tops are used to describe the science of turning objects in physics, however spinning tops are symmetrical and dancers' bodies are not. There will always be something that isn't symmetrical with a dancer, whether it be in the genes or by injury or habit. We must remember that bodies are not manufactured. Dancers, therefore, have to use their body in a balanced way.

Beginning right back with a baby's first crawling movement, the body uses balance to create movement. In the homolateral movement pattern there is an alternate movement outline. We can relate this to a turn that involves passé. Creating a balanced action between the passé leg and the arm on the opposing leg creates a centre of balance. *Dance Imagery for Technique and Performance* author Eric Franklin,[12] suggests that starting a class with doing a few crawling movements highly improves the coordination and balance of turns. One of my teachers' manual exercises for Level 1 turners involves some crawling and the coordination of crawl movement with the turn really emphasises to the youngsters the importance of using their torso to help them turn.

12   Franklin, E. (1996). *Dance imagery for technique and performance.* Champaign, IL: Human Kinetics.

I call this crossing abdominal action 'the seat belt' and use it to try and help dancers to find their midline of balance with the most symmetrical body that they can muster, that is without surgical operations! Although I wouldn't put that past some Dance Mums!

I believe that there is a difference between a turn and a spin and I believe that you can be a natural spinner. Similar to ice skaters, natural spinners often bring their foot nearer to their ankle in retiré and their supporting foot is on a very low demi-pointe. The modifications they make help them bring their body close to their turning axis making it much quicker and easier to turn. This is all fine, until you see them demonstrate a technical dance turn and it looks more like the Tasmanian Devil than a controlled pirouette.

Combining a dancer's natural spin with intense position focus will, in the end, create a fabulous turner, however 'spinners' need to focus extremely hard on approaching the turn in a calm fashion as opposed to doing as many as they can do. Imagine they are a coin flipping in slow motion; we need to actively see the front and the back of the dancer as they turn.

Something that dancers have different levels of is turning instinct, but as you'll see later on, turning instinct can be improved.

Scientific formulas complete, let's move on to…

2. COMMON FAULTS AND HOW TO REMOVE THEM

These subchapters are in the order of which are most important to me in pirouette teaching.

'The Sellotape Phenomenon'

Training the Position

'Muscles work in pairs' – that's the scientific part. While this next teaching method isn't filled with masses of scientific theory, it definitely works!

A Pirouette Surgery® workshop always begins with one child being taped up!

A few years ago, I was struggling with a child that would not stick her foot to her leg in pirouette position. It was hovering somewhere near, but no actual connection was happening and as a result the turn was about 30% effective, nowhere near the child's optimum potential. At the same time at the studio that I worked at, a duet was being rehearsed with two

The Selotape game

helium balloons. The best thing to keep them weighted down was, apparently, two little rolls of red tape. Now, the balloons didn't stay blown up for very long, so the rolls of tape were often on the desk waiting for the next balloon rehearsal. To cut a long story short (or should I say cut a long piece of tape shorter), instead of just using vocal correction and empty warnings of 'stick your foot on your knee or I'll stick it there for you', I actually got the tape and taped the child's foot in the correct position to her knee! I then made her stand there for about five minutes. Luckily we have very supportive parents at that school; the child wasn't allergic to the tape and the student actually enjoyed the whole process! The same child, from then on, always turns with her foot in a lovely position, and at aged nine, starts her jazz solo with a flawless quadruple pirouette!

Please don't think I advocate this as a good teaching method, however the visualisation and the taping made me really think.

Todd Hargrove,[13] author of *Better Movement* states, 'The bottom line is that posture is not a static position to be held, but rather a dynamic and constantly changing series of subtle movements'.

Positioning and posture when turning is so important. I like dancers to think of it as a position that is constantly moving rather than one that is static, however this is much harder to explain to children. When you say 'position' they automatically think 'statue', so trying to get a dynamic posture is tricky to say the least! However once the dancers know which muscles are those that need to keep engaging, as opposed to just being held motionless, the turns improve drastically. Dancers will go from looking stiff and wobbly to fluid and consistent. How a dancer feels whilst doing a movement is a parallel reflection to their improvement and I'm sure most of us prefer to feel fluid than stiff! For children, finding their balance is an ongoing exploratory process and striving for perfect, rigid balance too soon can interfere with

13   Hargrove, T. (2016). *Home*. [online] Better Movement by Todd Hargrove. Available at: http://www.bettermovement.org [Accessed 28 Jun. 2016].

the nervous system's automatic responses. I like young dancers to understand what muscles they are using in a dynamic posture so they can be creative problem-solvers with their balance and in the long run, create a stronger sense of balance. This is where I feel that dancers who have trained as gymnasts have an added advantage in turning, with finding and altering their balance. From a young age they are placed on a beam from which they do their absolute upmost not to fall off. We've all seen that moment when a gymnast performs a move and there is that moment of wobble whilst they attempt to regain their balance on the beam, working the abdominals left, right, forward and back. Whilst similar to dancers, in that gym coaches want their students to perform their moves without wobble, they also accept that it doesn't always go correctly and the athlete will need to be trained to save a movement if they so need to!

The Sellotape game at the start of a Pirouette Surgery® workshop in truth helps with two things. Firstly, breaking the ice, the children find it funny, but secondly, and most importantly, it starts the dancers subconsciously visualising the dynamic posture! Now, it isn't necessary to tape the dancers up at the start of every class, however picking a different place each time you focus on turns will soon make the dynamic posture, whilst creating a habit and therefore the successes of the rotations will improve.

I like to say that the two body parts have to work together, as opposed to imparting the anatomical details that are actually happening. We all know there is no muscle that joins your shoulder to your hip, however whilst turning, imagining that there is, really holds the connection of the dancer's core and also the positioning of the retiré leg.

Without using industrial-strength gaffer tape… try the following to engage your dancers' dynamic pirouette positions.

1. Hypothetical Circle of Steel (Literally – Circle of Sellotape)

We've all been told to imagine a wire between the fingers in en avant to help support the arms and give the connection between the two. Here is my first piece of tape; joining the fingers together with about two inches in between.

The dancers are now thinking of a constant flow of energy around both arms.

2. The Seat Belt

Using a body-length piece of tape, attach one end at the front hip bone of the lifted retiré leg and then stick the tape up the body to the opposite shoulder.

The dancers are now thinking of the diagonal core oblique muscle, balancing out any hip lift on the working side.

3. The Seat Belt becomes the X-Factor

Add an oppositional (to the seat belt) piece of tape crossing the body.

The dancers are now further engaging the core muscles and this helps eradicate any leaning back, which results in falling backward.

4. Foot Position

The original taping situation, taping the foot to the knee. In parallel, the tape wants to go around the toes' knuckles and around the bony part of the knee. In turnout, you have to get a bit more creative with your taping!

The squeezing of the toes to the knee activates the inner thighs, stabilising the pelvis and holding the leg in optimal position.

5. <u>What Goes Up Must Come Down!</u>

Always the funniest one for the children involved, taping their toes to the floor. Finding the push down as well as the pull up in the supporting leg. (There's loads more on this later on in the imagery section!)

Remember... If dancers push too hard into the floor they end up falling backwards. Use the floor instead as a support system. Feel its importance but don't push it away too much.

Quite simply, tape the toes to the floor!

6. <u>The Invisible Muscle</u>

This is only really accessible in the parallel retiré position. This is an invisible connection between the knee of the leg in passé and the wrists. Another great one to engage the core and also create correct proprioception of the body parts.

Tape from the top of the knee to the Circle of Steel.

7. <u>Wings</u>

It's always hard for a dancer to find and use their latissimus dorsi. I call them wings and many of the props I use are aids to help locate these seriously important muscles. Later on in the book I take you through how dancers can find their wings! Without moving the dancer's arm position, one assumes they have them in a nice and rounded #squeezethebeachball position, attach tape from each elbow to about the third rib under the armpit on each side. Now tell the dancer to wrinkle and then smooth this piece of tape by utilising their latissimus dorsi muscles. Don't let them flex their upper spines or lift their shoulders.

The dancer's arms and back are now stabilised and in a lovely strong position.

8. <u>Reverse X-Factor</u>

A lot of focus is on engaging the abdominal muscles but we don't want dancers to forget that this means the back too. Sometimes I let the dancers tape each other up and often when it comes to 'how can we engage the back muscles' they put tape across the upper back. This leads to pinching of the shoulder blades and often then causes a leaning back action. Taping from the shoulders to the opposing pelvis side, helps long, drawn down movements across the back, opening the chest and eradicating slumped posture. (Perhaps we should all tape ourselves up!)

Dancers are now engaging all their back muscles and the focus on core hasn't tripped them forward.

The taping posistions

Focusing eighty per cent of your pirouette class time on the importance of the posture and positioning of the turn, and the little bit left on the actual spinning, will improve your dancers' turns massively. That is if you can persuade them that the boring bit actually will help them! Remind them, you can't send a text message without learning the alphabet first!

The '5' Instructions

This is useful for more advanced dancers and I often use this if I have a class who have done the Pirouette Surgery® masterclass before.

There are five major muscle groups that I think, if instructed correctly, create the most perfect Pirouette Position, can you guess what they are?

Well? Try this and see how you feel!

1. Stand with your feet parallel and squeeze your inner thighs. (Muscle group 1- Adductors)
2. Draw one leg up to retiré keeping the inner thighs engaged and suck the the pelvic floor and transverse abdominis in and up (Muscle group 2- Transverse Abdominis)
3. Lift your arms to en avant and then pull the lats down to #findyourwings. (Muscle group 3- Latissimus Dorsi)
4. Connect the bottom of the lats to the obliques, therefore squeezing the abdominals in a diagonal way to join the tension in the lower abdominals. (Muscle group 4- Obliques)
5. Squeeze your bum as much a possible, stabilising the leg and also the pelvic area. (Muscle group 5- Gluteals)

Feeling strong? Dynamic? Prepared to turn? I am!

A *T.Rex* Can't Turn. Arms, Arms, Arms!

Arms are forgotten in technique and often a secondary thought, something used to decorate rather than mechanical.

I always say, as does Krista Miller, the position in a turn is the number one factor to making it successful or not. Included in the position of the body (as well as the legs and spine), are the dancers' arms. Arm positioning is one of the most important aspects to helping a dancer turn, both statically and also in travelling turns. Astonishingly, throughout my touring workshops, arms are the part of the position that need the most work as well as the part that has the most variations! Dance teachers in the UK do not necessarily have to have knowledge of the biomechanical functions of anatomy to be a qualified dance teacher, however I really wish that it were something that was included in the training. Knowing how a dancer can create a movement to be mechanically optimum is something I have really researched and have found priceless to my training of dancers. If dancers' arms are correctly placed then the power in the back, stability in the torso and strength in the core can be used to their best state. Arm placement is not only a superficial aesthetic in creating 'nice lines and shapes' but is integral to the success of many movements.

Correct mechanical use of a dancer's anatomy is invaluable to all kinds of teaching, not just turns.

Gabriela Banuet, Pilates master trainer and founder of Intense Dancers Project, told me why teachers knowing how bodies function is of high importance to her...

'I think it is important for every dance teacher to work with and train with bodies, to understand anatomy, how muscles, joints, bones, ligaments and connectivity tissue activate the muscles to start any amount of force necessary to start a move.

If the teacher understands the principles of the movement then it will be easier for them to teach every dancer the proper technique to every movement.

Biomechanics also helps to prevent injuries; a teacher's responsibility is to teach a class that is safe to prevent injuries.

When teachers understand how the body moves they can instruct the dancers to appropriately use their bodies and become the best dancers they can be.'

Upper body strength within dancers is a taboo subject. I often hear teachers moaning that their 'gymnastics' children have broad shoulders, however upper body strength, including scapula stability, shouldn't always lead to bulked up young dancers. Samuel Downing, personal trainer, tours with me on some of my workshops and works on dancer conditioning. Many places we attend like to boast about the amount of press-ups, planks or sit-ups their students can do. He, however, likes to take away the boastful repetitions and instead replace them with minimal repetitions of continual tension training with perfectly formed isolating movements. This way, muscles will not bulk but instead become lean and then accessible to be used in an efficient way for movements. Less is definitely more when it comes to isolated strengthening. I like dancers to think of their body as a car. You only want to use the fuel that you need and not waste fuel on gear changes and braking that you don't necessarily need to do. Dancers' arms are like a well working clutch and gearbox. Put them in the correct placement for the turn and they will work to a dancer's advantage; speeding them up, keeping them balanced and slowing them down when they need to, all with minimum movement and muscular change. I always see dancers not using their arms to their advantage, because I don't think that they know any better. It takes impeccable focus to keep arms in one position, especially when losing balance, as our natural instinct is to throw our arms out to help us balance.

Directly connecting to turns, arms are used for balance as well as positional support; they also have the ability to alter the speed (angular velocity) of the turns by their placement. In more complex turns the arms are added to the coordination of the movements and helps create further torque and momentum within the turns.

Placement

During a pirouette I teach that the arms should always be level with the sternum. One of the most common pirouette mistakes I see is where dancers hold their arms in a low first position, which destabilises the upper body and can make the dancer lose control quickly. This is controversial as some master trainers work in the opposite way, with the arms lower down by the belly button. Their argument for this is that for the weaker dancer, the higher up the arms come there is more likelihood of their shoulders lifting up and their upper back curving. In defence of my method; if the dancers have been taught the muscular awareness of the dynamic position (Selotape game) properly the hunching won't happen.

Pre-Pirouette

Another mistake I often see from dancers with their arms is that they wind up around the body, so often the arms move from a perfect preparation position across the midline of the body to try and create further force in the turn. I touch upon this again in the preparation section. This is all well and good if the dancer has an impeccably strong torso and complete control of their body when moving the arms and also finding the wind up within their deep abdominals too. Although 99% of the time, the dancers I have before me are not ones with the strong torso or muscular connection but ones that are just hoping for the best and have absolutely no idea that swinging the arms isn't going to help a turn.

Top Tip:

For the dancer described above (The arm-swinger) I usually use the 'seat belt drill'. Preparation for the turn is as normal but the arms are already in their perfect rounded position so the dancers must learn to engage the turn by using their core and back muscles as opposed to their arms. I often find here, that the turns when the dancers do not use their arms are much more technical, and also more consistent, than when they decide to fling their arms about! It also helps to stand to the side of a child when preparing and tell them that you are blocking their arm from moving behind peripheral vision and therefore being behind the side of them, and this doesn't allow any wind-up. For little dancers this is one of the most important parts of technique in the position of preparation, it is a natural movement to wind up but not one that can work

The Seat Belt

mechanically. I often use a foam roller for this too. As opposed to being hit in the stomach by overwinding ten-year-olds, I place the foam roller where I would stand. The slightest touch will knock it over... and so pirouette Skittles *was born!*

(I use the foam roller to help with leaps too... but that's a whole other story.)

Centrifugal and Centripetal Forces

I have decided that 'arms' is the most used word yelled across the room for me whilst I teach. Perhaps, I should get that tattooed on to me next! It is a constant struggle to get young dancers to use their arms consistently and to remember them when they are trying to do however many other things. Good arm placement with muscular understanding comes from repetition over many years of training. My extension programme dancers, finally (although now I've written this I am sure they will defy what I have stated) do use their arms to their advantage... now. It's taken four years to get it ingrained in their bodies, as well as intensive conditioning classes, so that the arms are beneficial to their movements. In a static position most dancers can demonstrate what good arm positioning is, and with the correct instructions and disciplines, practise the strength of these positions too, however, it does take a while for dancers to automatically use their arms properly. Once this does become habit the success, consistency and product of all dance moves, especially turns, become much greater. The additional problem for dancers and holding their positions is, as soon as they start turning the centripetal force (all objects that rotate have an inward pulling or pushing force, this force counteracts the desire for a moving object to travel in a straight line) begins to override the stable holding force of the muscles and often the harder and more times a dancer rotates, the harder it is to hold the position because of the amount of force asserted on to it by an external force. It's like when you're spinning on a Waltzer at a fairground, you can try and hold your body still but the intense centrifugal forces act and buffer your body so you cannot resist movement any longer.

In response to the inward force being place on the turning dancer, they will also experience the centrifugal force which counteracts the inwards centripetal force and this is the desire of the object rotating to travel forwards as opposed to in a straight line. Both of these forces create a substantially difficult condition for any moving object, an inanimate object has a hard enough time spinning with these external factors and that cannot change its position in anyway, just think how much more difficult it becomes when an animate object (a living, walking, talking dancer) experiences these forces. It is therefore imperative to train that dynamic posture. Whilst internally muscles are not solid and are constantly working to create a position that isn't stiff, it's important that whilst turning that position never changes. These external forces will override even the slightest twitch and send the pirouette into meltdown!

Chinese Whispers of Arm Positions

When giving workshops I try very hard to show that these are my ideas for optimum turning and not ones that are set in stone. The positioning of the arms changes between associations and exam boards, and often follows the Matt Mattox-inspired 'jazz port de bra' positions, as opposed to the arms that I find mechanically help turns the most. I do not aim to change the world (although that would be a good career aim), all I hope to do is to inform and help teachers and dancers progress. When it comes down to arm placement, I do not agree that the bent elbow, jazz first position is suitable to complete multiple turns and I am aware that this statement contradicts all British Modern dance syllabi. The jazz arm positions are derived from different jazz styles and choreographers and are altered stylistically to suit different choreographic styles. I find that these positions are more externally attractive than useful. My opinion is, and do remember everyone is entitled to an opinion... many dance syllabi in the UK teach routines that demonstrate movements; they are not however training exercises or drills. This is where the dance training of jazz in the UK differs hugely to the practices in the USA. I personally feel that dance training in the UK is sometimes limited due to time restraints of learning a syllabus and entering exams. Many schools lack time or staff to offer free work and that is where the leaps, turns and tricks are practised, drilled and perfected. Yes, I agree that not all good quality dances involve these 'competition' elements but as theatre and commercial dance is progressing, it is fortunately, or unfortunately, however you might look at it, changing how dance is presented. Modern dance here in the UK takes on a completely different meaning to what modern dance is in the USA. Modern to Americans is that of contemporary syllabi and creators, such as Horton, Cunningham and Graham etc. However modern to the UK is more along the lines of theatre and jazz. Although if we look at it like that why do our 'modern' classes not consist of the same things that USA jazz classes do? There's a lot of fogginess around the genres and differentiations of styles, however what is demonstrated in a syllabus modern class in the UK is based purely on stylistic and choreographic elements as opposed to training and drilling movements for consistency and perfection. Dance needs freedom of creativity and artistry, definitely, but dancers also need to know how to use their bodies properly. This not only makes the standard of dance higher, more impressive and intricate, but also eradicates injury and enhances safety within the dancers' bodies.

Going back to my point about arms, the arms that are used in syllabi are there for decoration and style (unfortunately a 1980's style too) but not put there for mechanics. Therefore I never ever teach arms for pirouettes in class with the bent elbow, I find it very hard to get children to engage their back muscles and use the arms to their advantage in the bent position. I find that it also throws a dancer's centre of gravity backwards, gives them the opportunity to throw their upper back backwards, which in turn distorts the spine and the pelvis region, and doesn't promote connection with the core. This arm line has been used for years for pirouettes here in the UK, but where it came from and why it is used isn't particularly clear to me. The position has been set in stone in a syllabus, and like sheep, we dance teachers have followed suit, taught it to pupils who in turn have taught it to other pupils. A cult of bent arm pirouettes, all because someone thought it looked different and interesting!

In contrast to this, I do not like to change a dancer's arm position if it is working for them. Similar to how this book highlighted Mikhail Baryshnikov's modifications to help his turns, some arm positions are altered by the dancers because they facilitate the turn better for their body shape. Some dancers successfully turn with their arms in a low bra bar position. I describe this as 'Balanchine-y' and some also happily rotate numerous times with the arms in the above-stated bent position. These dancers are rare to find and often very advanced. It is more likely that improving a dancer's arm position to the shape I promote in a Pirouette Surgery® class will be more beneficial to the consistency and amount of turns than substantiating the idea above, that different arm positions work for different people.

There are then the dancers that do not use their arms at all, either keeping them down by their sides, or doing some strange crossed over, weak, *T.Rex*-style arm positioning. Not using your arms on purpose and keeping them down by your sides whilst turning can be valuable to pirouette training, as it enhances and highlights the importance of using the shoulders and torso to stimulate the turn. However using the arms in a weak position or a position that alters every time will only highlight the vulnerability and inconsistency of the turns. Weakness in any part of the body will cause a domino effect and then diminish the strength throughout the whole body. *Try and engage your lats but let your core hang out; pretty difficult really.*

Position Evaluations

Position	Pros	Cons
	Position for turns recognised by most UK Dance Associations.	-Ribs are open so weight leaning back. By leaning the top of the spine back the pelvis is tilted forward and back is arched. Allowing weak core control. -Little scapula or back muscle control is shown.
	Recognised ballet position. For the stronger dancer this position allows a prettier and aesthetically pleasing balletic style.	-Elongated arms often lead the body to fall forward, by pulling the head and shoulders forward out of alignment. -To engage back muscles sometimes this position allows shoulders to lift.
	Helps dancers keep their shoulders down. Good for engaging shoulders and lats. -Often varied by arms twisting wrists underneath.	Lacks circular shape for all-round balance. Moment of inertia is small so speed will be fast at start of turn. Panto dame cupping-of-boobs springs to mind… Never a good idea with kids…!

The table above highlights three common turning positions with the arms. None of which are what I teach as the most mechanically optimum, due to their placement in proportion to the turning axis.

The next image below highlights the relationship the arms have to the turning axis and the most optimum shape to aid their aerodynamic and balance qualities. The X is the axis and the green line the shape.

The orbits of the arms and their turning axes

The most mechanically efficient position that I preach is as follows;
A ballet first position, lifted towards the height of the sternum and bent in 40%. (Imagine that 0% is them in a long first position, 100% is them bent right in, touching the chest.) Lats engaged and pulling down. Chest open.

That or... pretend you are this emoji.

Arm placement Emoji

True, this icon has exceedingly short arms, one I hope that your dancers don't have, but relating a position to something that is on trend will always solidify what you are aiming for. Plus pretend to be her; she's holding her head with hands close together but not touching and her elbows are bent, now bring those arms down level with your sternum but don't change their shape. Et voila!

Arm Imagery

There are many images that can be used to help dancers create a suitable arm position. I personally favour this one: the cone. The dancers need to imagine the shape they make in the air, not so much the static position, but the position that would be drawn by the body throughout the turn. This imagery helps keep the arms high and rounded and helps dancers feel the whole turn. Keeping the main mass of the turn higher creates a spinning top shape with the spine as the spinner and the main turning axis.

From the images earlier you can see that the cone theory doesn't work with other arm positions discussed. If a spinning top were made with any of these proportions then it would not be equally balanced and would fall over. The exact same theory applies to pirouettes. You can use hoops with your dancers to demonstrate these actions.

Cone Theory

Conservation of Angular Momentum with Arm Positions

An object of constant mass will spin faster when the radius is smaller. So in a turn, the smaller the circle with the arms, the faster and easier pirouettes become. It is also important that the dancer is aerodynamic, that the turning position limits restrictions and that the air around the dancer is not interrupted abruptly. Therefore, a curved arm position will glide around in the air as opposed to a bent position with the elbows causing restriction.

#FindYourWings – Training For Good Arm Placement

Samuel Downing, personal trainer, spends a lot of time during his conditioning classes helping dancers 'find their wings' (i.e. engage their latissimus dorsi and stabilise their scapulas). For children, finding these muscles is tricky, because at first they lift their shoulders, which is exactly the muscle memory we do not want for pirouettes! As always, relating this to something childlike will help.

Darcie gained her wings

Automatically engaging your lats to help a movement doesn't come easy, it's hard to get dancers to use their muscles automatically without reminders. Therefore it is important to focus on the important parts right from the very start. We as dance teachers don't get much more than ten years between primary and dance college (and that's if the students don't give up, change dance schools or take up fencing) to train our students to the best they can be before they move onwards and upwards. Training young dancers to perform complex movements in a mechanical way should start young with constant reminders of the technical elements. This gives them the best chance possible to train their bodies and know how to use them, in turn creating stronger and efficient dancers. I am not saying quit picking flowers with your baby class, or ban recreational classes and focus purely on technique, as you will lose students like that. You need to find the balance between teaching students to use their bodies like athletes and also have fun!

My little dancers gain their wings! When I see some good turns with engaged lats and stable shoulders they then get to wear the fairy wings. Teachers you've all got a set of fairy wings kicking around in the costume cupboard, probably somewhere between the clown outfits, cowboy hats and cat ears! (Purposeful alliteration? Who knows!) I've not tried this with bigger kids, but they probably would love it just as much!

Don't however give your students the wings and then expect them to turn. Adding them to their backs will affect their centre of gravity, add air friction... and likely they'll lose their wings way quicker than they gained them!

Arm Additions for Beginner Turners - Magnet Hands!

Any teacher would understand the problems in facing a junior ballet class and attempting to get them to keep their arms in a first position whilst moving through a dance move; you know the placement is unlikely to stay perfect. That is if you can even get it perfect whilst the little dancers are static! Proprioception in little dancers can be very distorted and, with their arms playing such an important role in the process of their pirouette success, I have a little tool that helps them create the correct muscle memory position of their arms.

In the studios that I teach, once your ninth birthday arrives, 'magnet hands' are taken away. You want to use this tool long enough to gain the understanding but not too long to ingrain a bad technique, especially if the children find it hard to differentiate this position to the one needed in the ballet class.

When turning, ask the dancers to place their knuckles in the palm of the opposite hand, joining the first position together. By doing this the dancers can feel the connection between the arms and the position, as well as engaging their backs and core.

However some of my dancers have 'big' turns in their solos and sometimes I see magnet hands employed as a safety net, when nerves or the prizes at stake are high!

Advanced Arm Alterations to Improve Turning

Pace

Using the arms to aid the pace of the turn is quite an advanced procedure, but pure pirouette magic when it works! Alexander Campbell, RBC, is the first person that I noted successfully using this, but since having it highlighted to me, many professional dancers and competent turners use this to enhance their turns.

'The Campbell Technique' (as my dancers began to call it after I told them about this!). This is specifically for advanced turners, who want to integrate further rhythmic practice into their turns.

Whilst watching a Royal Ballet pre-performance class, I couldn't help but notice Alexander Campbell's slightly abnormal use of arms in his phenomenal pirouettes! Six or seven rotations every time and he wasn't really trying either. As he turned, his arms moved smoothly through á la seconde towards his first/en avant position. During my interview with him, which can be found in my chapter 'Let's Talk Turns', he mentioned that this helped with the pace and rhythm of his turns, and sure enough it does help stabilise and also helps add those few extra rotations in the big numbered turns.

The position of your body can help speed things up or slow things down, this is apparent in pirouettes as much as it is in everyday life. Take an office chair for example. Sit in the chair with your feet off the ground and extend your arms out whilst someone else gives you a little spin. Slowly bring your arms in and watch what happens to the speed of your turn.

Scientifically, when you are rotating, you've got a quality called angular momentum, which depends on your angular velocity (your speed around the circular motion), and a quantity called moment of inertia. This measures how much your body will resist a change in angular velocity and it's related to how your mass is distributed. Consequently, moving your arms in and out changes your moment of inertia.

Angular Momentum = Angular Velocity x Moment of Inertia

However for us laymen of science in the dance world, this means:

When your arms are out wide you will spin slower than you will when your arms are pulled in tight!

When the moment of inertia decreases the angular velocity (speed) must increase to balance out the momentum.

This is what Campbell uses to find the rhythm of his multiple turns, starting perhaps with the first and second turn in á la seconde and then drawing in slowly to an en avant position for turns three, four and five. This can be taken even further, and is often observed with younger dancers from the USA, closing the arms in even further, still rounded but with the wrists and forearms crossed. By crossing the arms and making the shape even smaller it lessens the moment of inertia and makes the turn faster.

Moving the arms from a wide position into a tighter one during the rotations helps keep the pace and stability of the turn. It also helps gather velocity as the moment of inertia decreases, so the turns speed up, allowing the body to have enough momentum for further rotations. Coordinating the arms throughout the turn takes a lot of skill and I would only advise adding it once other anomalies within the technique have been eliminated. This process uses the formula for angular momentum and decreases the moment of inertia by bring the position closer to the turning axis.

Using your parachute

Opening the arms out at the end of a turn to slow down and secure the finish is a lovely addition for the advanced turner. It does take a lot of coordination and practice. A similar arm action happens at the end of a posé turn sequence, with the 'up, up, finish', but we all know how hard that is to eradicate the little hop and slowly lower to the fourth! This is another process that uses moment of inertia theory by increasing it in order to lose velocity. A definite and asserted movement of the arms will create this action, yet if the action is too strong it will throw the dancer's weight backwards. Again, I stress, this is something I only add for the most advanced turners.

Upper Body Strengthening Exercises

Shared by Samuel Downing, personal trainer and dance conditioning specialist*

All exercises must be supervised and practised after a full warm up.

Location

First of all dancers need to locate the muscles that need to be used. Sam likes dancers to sit in pairs, cross-legged, one in front of the other, with arms and hands out like a fork. This we call lumière position. It is advised to give a visual demonstration of where they need to feel the contraction and ask them to imagine a bodybuilder in front of them, seeing massive muscular triangles coming from their armpits. He then gets the dancers to squeeze down to the floor. It is important to learn that this isn't shoulder isolation, so that the dancers do not lift their shoulders up and down. The partner behind uses two fingers to try and feel if the dancers can isolate the muscles. Whatever the age, this is a fabulous exercise for muscle awareness.

Samuel Downing locating latissimus dorsi in lumiere position

Strengthening the Latissimus Dorsi

In the same position as above, the partner stands up and holds on to the other's hands. The dancer then pushes down with a controlled tension and importantly, no locked elbows. They then work simultaneously with a pushing down and up action. They feel the latissimus dorsi pushing, contracting downwards and then this stabilises the upper body and lifts the chest.

Exersise 1

Lumière pulses

- Arms forked, four small pulses of lats up and down, in 1 count.
- Reach up and then pull down on the strings four times, in 2 counts. *The arms then come to á la seconde so they can relate it to dance.*
- Repeat small pulses of lats in this position
- From ballet fifth to second pull downs. Four sets of each.

Repeat the same from ballet first and then moving to á la seconde and out.

Exersise 2

(Strengthening the upper body and arms.)

<u>Continuous Tension Press-Ups</u>

Continuous tension is good because it fatigues the muscle quicker and traps the blood in the muscle to make it stronger in a more efficient time frame. It makes the muscles work aerobically and improve endurance. This helps the dynamic postures of pirouettes.

Technique Notes

Box Press-Up – Knees and feet are on the floor, hands slightly wider than shoulders.

Half Press-Up – Knees slide back, so knees, hips and shoulders are in a straight line.

Correct box press-ups for young dancers

NB: Only teenager (fore mostly boys) should attempt full press-ups. Children's skeletons are still developing. They cannot handle the stress of pressing body weight and may be easily injured.

Make sure that...

1. Abdominals are braced the whole time.
2. Build up to doing three minutes.
3. Wrists must be underneath shoulders.
4. No hunching, keep the chest lifted.
5. Make sure breathing is correct. 'In' as you go down and 'out' as you push back up.

Goal: a three-minute long track.
Working through a series of five different tempo styles of press-up.

*   Four x four counts down and four counts up.
*   Four x three down and one up.
*   Four x two down and two up.
*   Eight x single count up and down.
*   Drop and Stop – down halfway then two counts to push back up. Drop one, hold one, and push up two.
*   Keep repeating; take a short break in between the sets.

Traditional press-ups are elbows out however, for Sam's exercise, elbows should go diagonally back and down, so there is more tension in the lats and the chest as opposed to working the triceps and biceps.

These can be repeated with triceps-style press-ups.

It is important as a dancer to strengthen both opposing arm muscle groups; these should be balanced for optimal performance and to minimise injury.

The Instagram Posture

Whilst the children I teach probably don't sit in an office all day, their posture, upper back and neck placement isn't optimum with their slouching at school and incessant use of mobile phones!

Strengthening the back opens the chest. The back is the most important part to strengthen in order to maintain good posture. General environmental factors from being on phones, watching TV and sitting in cars for long periods of time, naturally allows your chest to cave in, thus shortening the muscles in the front and stretching your back muscles. We need to counterbalance this by strengthening the back and stretching the chest.

Exersise 3

<u>Insta-Rows</u>

Wide and narrow arm rows with a Thera-Band connected to a fixed point.

+ 'Y-rows'
Hands are shoulder height and they come up to a Y, like the YMCA dance. This works the rhomboids and the trapezius.

Eight - 12 repetitions and three – four sets. Sixty second rest between each set.

Props

As an alternative to these specific exercises, you can squeeze something to engage your lats and this also helps focus on the core control. I sometimes like dancers to practise single pirouettes holding the objects, starting with it in the preparation front arm, as it really gives a connection straight away to the turn. Applying your imagery and drills to the actual turn, as opposed to just the static positions, is highly important. As teachers, sometimes our only focus is to get the positions perfect before the children even move. Firstly, this is boring for the kids, but more importantly, it doesn't represent the actual movement and the likelihood is that it will be a completely different matter when the dancer tries to apply the correction or the idea to the rotating movement.

You can get your dancers to squeeze anything! Ideally choose an item designed for this resistance, e.g. a Pilates ring, or a Pilates ball. Other things that I have been known to use are yoga blocks, tap shoes, teddy bears, literally whatever you can find in the studio! Alexander Campbell mentions in his interview that he was given a character shoe to hold when practising his turns as a child.

Quoits

As well as helping to engage back muscles, holding a lightly weighted object in your hands whilst turning allows the turner to feel the momentum of the turn better; it allows you to feel the rotation as opposed to a spin. I chose school plastic quoits, because of the circular shape they are

Props to activate proper use of arm and back muscles.

easier to grab hold of, but it can be anything that is used. By grabbing hold of something from the first whip of the arm it really helps the dancer coordinate the arms to their advantage. You can also use these in á la seconde turns to aid coordination, by swapping the quoit from hand to hand during each open and close.

The quoit also represents a steering wheel. It's important to keep it in front of the chest or you would veer off of the road! They eliminate twisting of the torso before and whilst turning.

Thera-Band Handcuffs

Many dancers do not use their backs and much of the arm placement in a pirouette relies solely on well placed connection between the back muscles to the core. You can buy leg resistance bands that simulate an oversized rubber band and can be used for leg strengthening. However, inventive as I am, I created a new use for them! Loop the band around your wrists in a figure of eight, place your arms in an en avant rounded position and pull, engaging your lats first, your arms a little way apart. This has the desired effect rather fast! You can even prepare for the pirouette (obviously there can be no wind up with the arms either, so it's a good training exercise for torso turning too!) with the band slack and then stretch it during the turn. Couple of minutes with the band, and then without and the arm placement is already much, much better.

It is interesting to note to your dancers that many of the exercises that help their turns are connected to using their back muscles. Similar to the glutes, the back and its muscular connections are the most forgotten, yet a vitally important part of a dancer's body. In leaps, adage and especially turns, dancers that involve their back strength in the moves are much more consistent. Perhaps it is because dancers can't see their backs when they're dancing, but it is an important part for us teachers to remind them how important it is. The back completes the core area for stability. You can describe to your students that they are in a tube, this highlights to them the whole circumference of core stability and all parts of their body are connecting and engaging to touch each side of the tube. I also like dancers to connect their upper and lower torsos, firstly by the Lego bricks mentioned later but secondly by asking them to imagine that they have two plaits hanging down (these would be their trapezius muscles) and they have been joined right down at the arch of their back with a strong hair tie, this is then connecting their trapezius right down into their core back muscles. Not only does this keep the dancers' shoulders down but also engages their back with their front core.

The arm positions that I promote will enhance both jazz and balletic pirouettes. Once choreography has begun, the placement of the arms can change and be used to decorate. An advanced dancer should be able to engage their back and core without the use of their arms in front of them. Do remember when choosing arms to decorate turns that arms are used for two things; balancing out a position and also creating a position that is aerodynamic. Always imagine that you are swimming before adding an arm line that causes your body to gain drag friction in the air; that is unless you want to slow down!

Spaghetti Legs- Leg Positioning

I'm always eating, yet always hungry and whilst writing this book I realised how many of my images that I use for dancers are centred around food! My two favourite imageries for legs include:

Spaghetti Legs

We don't want cooked spaghetti legs, then they'd be all wobbly and weak! If you like to analyse everything, then true, we don't really want uncooked spaghetti either, as then it would be brittle, but six-year-olds associate the two types of spaghetti with wobbly and strong!

Happy Knees

There is absolutely no point telling little ones to pull up their quadriceps muscle! Instead, I love the Happy Knees analogy, as do my students, and the seniors too. When you pull up your quads, the top of your knee area lifts like a smile! Many a student of mine has gone home with penned on smiley faces on their knees!

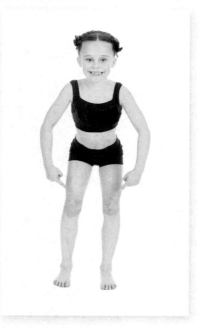

This correction, vitally important to turns, is the elongation and strength in the supporting leg. Again, similarly to arms, it's something that we can get so perfect on dancers at the barre and statically, and then as soon as they start moving, it is forgotten about.

Strength, and a straightened underneath leg, comes with time and good teaching, as well as muscular understanding and proprioception, and with a 'sprinkling' of good flexibility. Tight hamstrings limit

Happy Knees

how straight a leg can be, especially when the pelvis is also in neutral.

'Pull up your legs', can mean a vast amount of things to a young dancer. Paying very close attention to their knees throughout their training and especially in growth spurts is highly important. Sway backs and locking can cause injury and pain.

Whilst a little sway back looks lovely in an arabesque line, the actual health of the knee joint does get forgotten. It is so important for dancers to understand that pulling up their knees actually involves their quadriceps, hamstrings and inner thigh muscles (which when they are hypermobile and very flexible is a very tricky one to isolate.) It is a supporting action, as opposed to a locking action. I like dancers to imagine that their kneecap is a toy in an arcade machine and the muscles around it are the claws of the machine grabbing and lifting it up. If one claw does not close and lift then the toy falls out. Linking to dance, if one muscle doesn't join in, the joint will not be stable.

Pirouettes involve massive amounts of leg strength; both the strong and sustained action of holding the body up on relevé and the fast twitch action of using the power stored in the fast preparation to accelerate the turn. The legs are the part connected to the floor and they are the part that creates the initial torque and position, therefore strong lean legs are 100% needed to show consistent and perfect pirouettes.

The Michael Jackson

Taken too literally this does not aid turns, as it tilts the pelvis all out of place! However, I like to use Michael Jackson's hip thrust image to fire up dancer's glutes. By locking the glute into place at the top of the strong leg, it creates a solid and completed position of the whole leg. Many teachers like to say to engage the glutes forward to stabilise that area. Forward may be the wrong word scientifically, as they cannot isolate in space, but the image of keeping that hip and glute forward helps the dancer completely align their pelvis over the supporting foot, therefore creating a perfect turning axis. This is particularly useful in balletic turned out turns. You can also get your dancer to slide their hand down as they turn and push the supporting hip forward. I call this 'ASDA price'! (Although it appears that this isn't part of that supermarket's advertisement campaign any more!)

The Working Leg

We spend a lot of time focusing on the supporting leg, but the working leg that lifts to retiré can play a big part in the failure of a turn too. If, when a dancer lifts their leg to retiré, their hip lifts too, this will throw the dancer's torso out of alignment. The focus on getting the thigh bone parallel to the floor and coming straight out from the hip is highly important, as is that both hips are completely level next to each other. (This is for parallel jazz turns.)

I like to tell my dancers that the hip socket is relaxed and the thigh bone is floating there without any tension. Unless a dancer has very tight hips, then most dancers will be able to lift their retiré leg to the correct angle from the hip. Once the hip flexor area tenses and lifts, the pelvis is then also out of alignment, making the dancer's abdominal muscles work even harder to maintain a straight torso. If the hip lifts the torso will shift and the axis for the turn will have a kink it in, therefore not an optimum axis.

Young dancers automatically lift their hip because they think that that is where the bending action comes from. It is important to spend time on allowing the dancers to feel the difference between the two positions (lifted and level) so that they can see that actually the wrong, lifted position requires much more muscle tension than the one that is biomechanically optimum. The older dancers get, the more they must learn that the lifting action comes from their hamstring and glute, and it is vital for these muscles to engage, in order to maintain the retiré in the correct place. If you tell the dancers to lift the foot instead of their leg this also helps them keep their hips level. Also using the imagery of a tray balancing on their thigh bone, if it's at any angle other than straight out from the hip, everything will spill off of the tray!

A low thigh angle from the hip will also mean that the dancer's foot that should be connected to the side of the knee, will slip behind and often sickle while it's there. This time even without lifting the hips, the torso's alignment will have changed, as the lower retiré leg will mean that the pelvis must tilt forward to compensate for the knee's gravitational downward force. In Pirouette Surgeries, turns have massively improved when the dancers found that lift in their retiré.

The core exercises featured in this book will help with the dancer's understanding of how their core works and strengthen their ability to hold their pelvis in a neutral alignment. I like to focus, when dancers first practise their pirouette position, on the alignment of their pelvis. As many teachers have done before, I use the analogy of the pelvis being a bowl. I then like the dancers to metaphorically fill the bowl with their favourite beverage and then remind them not to spill it. It started off with a little slogan 'Don't spill your wine', but as the students I taught got younger it became 'Don't spill your Fanta'.

On Fondu or Not

A successful turn of any object depends purely on its turning axis. A dancer's turning axis is their spine and down their supporting leg. As mentioned in the arms section, the weight must be surrounding the axis evenly to maintain balance and not affect the velocity of the turn by sourcing drag from the air.

Historically, jazz turns have been taught and demonstrated on a low level. It is assumed that these are easier for the learning dancer. I like to contradict this point, as I personally feel that they are harder. Whilst a beginner dancer may not have the strength to fully pull up their leg when they turn and it be a little bent when they are rotating, this isn't the same idea as the set exercises in many syllabi demonstrate, when the turn must be shown on a forced arch relevé with the leg in a deep fondu position.

The reason I think that these are harder when demonstrated in the correct deep position, is that the dancer must use their body's muscle awareness to counterbalance the fact that the knee is adding weight to the front of the turning axis. By doing this, the dancer must lean back slightly to offset the resulting weight difference. If a dancer bends the retiré leg too much as well as the other leg on fondu, especially if they are tight in the hamstrings, the lumbar spine will contract under and create a warped turning axis. Often a 'bent' leg to a dancer doesn't necessary mean an engaged leg. It is only once a dancer is older, and has more intellect regarding how the body moves, that they can differentiate that a bent leg can also be engaged and strong. To maintain a forced arch position in pirouette requires a high level of strength, which is not developed in the preparation exercises for these bent leg turns.

The turning axis and its deviation for fondu turns

Therefore, I always teach pirouettes on a high level. Only once a high level turn is perfected, with understanding of weight placement, bodily counterbalance and engagement of all muscles in the leg, do I then begin to alter the fondu on the underneath leg, sometimes playing with straight and bent levels, down to the floor and then rising back up to high level to stop. These are highly advanced moves, not something we should teach when our dancers first meet pirouettes. I personally feel that it gives them bad habits and doesn't allow them to explore what a turn should really feel like.

'Heeling it'

(Sophia used that phrase. I'm *down* with the cool kids...)

My biggest observation of turning dancers is that they often let their heel drop down from their highest relevé. Whilst we automatically assume that this is down to their foot and ankle strength (which does play an important part) the heel going down is a knock-on effect. As soon as the core loses its posture, the pelvis alters its alignment, often losing glute control, and the leg has to change how it is holding a dancer on its axis as the heel goes down to counterbalance the booty sticking out! So, once again, like everything to do with our bodies and movement, the success of a turn on a high relevé is first and foremost reliant on good posture.

Hard Ankle

A strong leg would be completely useless if the extremity of it was weak. Strong ankles and feet are a massive positive to any dancer and dance move, but being able to use the strength in the ankle for turns is imperative.

Getting a dancer to their highest demi-pointe is unique to all, every dancer's feet are different; some have long toes, some have short; some have wide feet; flat feet; high arches; long or short Achilles. Physicality makes a big difference to the appearance and also efficiency of a dancer's demi-pointe.

What we must try and achieve, in all turning positions, is the highest demi-pointe possible for each individual dancer.
There has been a rise of foot torture devices arriving on the market. When I assess students' feet, a lot of them have more range than they can use, so focus is always on strengthening their range and often as this improves the foot flexibility does too. Any attempts to increase pointe range should

be done very slowly and with careful thought to the anatomy of the ankle to keep it stable and strong. Overstretched ligaments reduce alignment awareness, so in actual fact those dancers that have beautifully loose feet often find it hard to get up on a strong relevé.

Sometimes a dancer's feet can be quite strong and also their ankle flexible, but still they don't seem to be able to feel their highest demi-pointe. This is where the 'hard ankle' comes in. I like to say to dancers that their heel bone is going to push through the front of their ankle and by doing that the ankle becomes extra strong because it has the heel bone helping it too.

By doing this the dancer shifts their COG completely over the standing point of contact, as pushing the heel forward increases the engagement of the back of the leg leading up the glute, therefore stabilising the pelvis and overall the core. Good toes and naughty toes, or as I call them, 'toe sit-ups', have never been more important!

Another great exercise, to work on the highest possible rise, involves some yoga blocks. As long as the child's foot isn't too small, place the block underneath the demi-pointe position (use a barre to start with) and then push the ankle forward and rise higher off the block. Dancers straight away realise how lazy their relevé is and it also impacts the use of the back of the leg and glutes.

It is important to remember how many different foot types there are and important as a teacher to remember this when pushing dancers to their optimum demi-pointe. I have noticed around the country that some dancers often turn very well on a lower demi-pointe. The dancer's heels are about an inch off the floor, but they are getting multiple turns. This is extremely hard to change if the dancer has formed this habit when learning to turn. These dancers are often those that have worked tirelessly strengthening their feet, sometimes those who are not blessed with that 'ooh feet' reaction and they may have less flexible toes and physically cannot get so high up on demi-pointe. Now if the hard ankle analogy doesn't work with these dancers and they physically cannot get any higher then leave it at that and continue to stretch and condition the feet. If the dancers can find more in the flexion of the ankle, it is imperative that teachers focus on kicking the low heel habit (see my 'Kicking the Habit' section) in order to strengthen the straight line down the back of the body forming the vertical turning axis. Whilst turning in ballet shoes or jazz shoes, dancers can get away with that low relevé, it is going to be virtually impossible to progress on to a pointe shoe. Tap dancers often turn lower on the relevé, highly likely because their shoes don't bend as much!

Simple Leg Strengthening Exercises
Shared by Samuel Downing, Personal Trainer

Developing leg strength will help dancers have more efficient turns and stable preparation. Increasing leg strength will increase the amount of turns demonstrated by the application of torque from the legs and feet on the floor. Strong and engaged inner thighs and hamstrings help turns. These muscles connect to the base of the core and stabilise the leg. If dancers think of their thigh bone directly above the heel it straightens the turning axis.

Alternating forward lunges

These exercises develop power within the legs by repeating a series of lunges, using body weight resistance, developing quad, hamstring and glute strength as well as muscle memory in the preparation position.

Travel these across the room. Lunge to standing positions.

Pointers:
- Nice straight back.
- Front thigh parallel to the floor.
- Ankle must be underneath the knee and shin bone completely vertical.
- Back leg is bent.

Energy must be driving through the front foot on each stand up, which then can be developed into driving it through the ball of the foot for more advanced dancers when this exercise is taken to retiré position on relevé.

Stepping on to a chair or step

Engages quads and glutes. The weight transfers forwards, developing strength and power in the legs. This exercise helps dancers feel the driving force down and connection to the floor. It also engages their abdominals and enhances their ability to balance. Another way to emulate this action is to push up from kneeling to the pirouette position. It is good for dance teachers to observe good tracking of the knee in this position and make sure it always goes directly forward over the toes. It is advisable to start these exercises with a partner spotting for safety.

Glute and hamstring isolations

Glute muscles are highly important for the success and consistency of good posture. Strong glutes help keep the pelvis in alignment and support the legs and lower back, helping reduce the risk of injury from increased stretching and flexibility. Glutes are often something that dancers forget to focus on, but something teachers always ask dancers to squeeze. I find it important for dancers to know the locations of their glute muscles and discover ways to isolate and engage them that don't require 'squeezing' or even more detrimental to posture control, 'tucking under'. Increased strength throughout these muscle groups will improve a dancer's jumps and turns.

Oysters

These help with pelvic stability and back of leg muscle activation. These also develop turnout range.

Start lying on the side, with the underneath arm extended with the head resting. The top hand is bent in front of your shoulder. Hips are stacked directly on top of each other and knees are bent but drawn forward. Heels are in line with back and hips.

To initiate the movement the heels squeeze together so that the calves, glutes and hamstrings are pre-activated. Keeping this tension, you open your top knee as far as your hip range will let you without the hips tipping back. Children need to be carefully observed doing this as the movement is less than they think.

Carry out for ten repetitions.

Variations of timing:
- Ten – four counts up, four counts down.
- Three counts up, one down.
- One up and three counts down.
- Up for one and hold for seven.
- Singles, up one, down one.

Common mistakes to observe:
- Shoulder need to stay stacked.
- The hips shouldn't rock from side to side.

Bungee Kicks
Requires a looped band.
Starting on all fours, the band is wrapped around the thighs just above the knees, hands underneath shoulders and knees under hips.
Nice flat back and abdominals pulled in.

Lift right knee bent, level with hip alignment. Hips are square.
Tiny pulses lifting up and down. Don't let the knee drop below the hip.

Speed variations:
- Slow – two up and two down, for eight sets.
- Medium – one up and one down for eight sets.
- Fast – pulsing up the whole time.

Shoulder bridges

These are the best glute exercises for generating power from the preparation position up to the pirouette balance.

Don't confuse this with shoulder bridges for abdominals where you tilt the pelvis and roll through the spine. As you want to target the explosive plyometric power of the glutes, you don't need to roll through the spine on the way up. The abdominals must be braced so that no stress is put on the lower spine.

Movement description:
- Lying on the back, feet parallel and bring the heels right in.
- Relax the upper body with the hands beside you.
- Push the heels into the floor – calves, hamstrings and glutes activate.
- Drive up through the hips so the body is in a diagonal line.
- Roll back down through the spine.

Timing – up for one count and down for three. Ten times, three sets. Shake the legs out and glute stretch in between.

If you want to make this harder:
Hands up in the air, pressing and lifting the heels up so there is more calf action.

Lying hamstring sequence

This is excellent to engage the hamstrings solely. All the body weight is facing down and gravity is pulling the leg towards the earth.

Movement description:
Lying on your front, place your legs into a V-shape. Feet are turned out. Lift up the right leg, and keeping it turned out, engage the hamstring.

Exersise example;
- Pulse it ten times.
- Miniature circles, five each way.

- Flex the foot to bend and stretch the lifted leg.
- Bend 90 degrees and push the ceiling away with the foot.

Hips must stay pushed into the mat.

Repeat right and left legs.

Inner thigh strengtheners

There is a whole series of inner thigh exercises that dancers use that can be replicated from Pilates or toning classes.

These are the best exercises for young dancers to feel the connection of their inner thighs to their transversus abdominis… which in turn improves connections within their retiré position.

Movement description:

Lie the dancers on their backs and get them to bend their knees in, feet on the floor. From there tell them to squeeze their inner thighs together, at the same time they need to lift their pelvic floor muscles in and up also. Holding this and making sure the dancers are breathing for up to three minutes will really ingrain the lower connection in their turns.

Kinetic Leg Resistance Bands

My dancers and Sam use these bands regularly in our classes and we have been lucky enough to establish a connection with www.myosource.com and www.elitegymnastics.co.uk to offer readers of this book a 15% discount code 'rrosina' to buy this specific equipment.

Using the kinetic leg bands is one of the best ways for dancers to increase their speed, strength and explosive reactions. Adding resistance into your lower body movements not only strengthens but also activates the fast twitch muscle fibres. This method of training for power or explosiveness has been termed 'plyometrics'. The unique design of MyoSource leg resistance bands allows dancers aged seven years and upward to move unrestricted and in a natural manner, with full range of motion, so you can get stronger while working to improve sport-specific skills. It is important that dancers order the specific bands that compliment their age and weight to avoid injury.

All strengthening exercises, as well as ballet barre and some dance exercises, can be completed with these bands on.

With all resistance exercises, be wary of the age of the dancer and give younger students more rest time and progress the exercises week by week.

MyoSource Kinetic Bands

Bulky vs Lean

It's important not to engage the quads too much. Apart from the alternating lunges, Sam really focuses on the backs of the legs. He encourages elongated and extended exercises and never fatigues dancers by working them so hard as to cramp up, as this is when the muscles begin to bulk.

Sam tries to work the micro muscles rather than the powerhouse muscles, by taking exercises from Pilates and barre work as opposed to mainstream workout methods.

It is about the range of movement being smaller rather than extended; we know that the dancers are flexible. He works against their hypermobility. He does not use leg weights for children; body weight exercises should be fine.

He suggests that dancers do high intensity workouts and not long distance running. Running for long periods bulks muscles.

He prefers to use speed and agility, improving dancers' reaction time, something that is massively useful when needing to employ the muscles for a power preparation in a fast pirouette.

The Goldilocks Complex!

Diagrams highlighting inadequate preparation positions.
The pink dashed line is their turning axis. The Pink X's are their COG.

Preparation!

It's too wide... It's too thin...
It's too slow... It's too fast...
Ah... Just right!

Too Slow

The success of every turn hangs on that split second of preparation! Does anyone else have dancers who seem to do really lovely multiple turns in their lyrical solo, but seem to struggle for consistency in a class, drill-like situation?

Yes, I do! It's very unlikely (unless your choreography needs surgery too, but that's a whole other story, or should I say book; I hope to carry on the Surgery series!) that in the routine the dancer dégagés, prepares to jazz fourth and then sits stagnantly in that preparation for a few seconds before turning. It is likely during the dance there is a step, or a split second preparation that has to happen on a certain piece of music, often working with bodily momentum.

I am all for using the power in the legs, getting the most out of a dancers' plié, but training for more than just double pirouettes demands a more structured preparation involving a fast twitch contraction, not thighs of steel.

Aerobic and strength training in childhood have an impact on the amount of fast and slow twitch fibres that we have. Hereditarily our bodies are more suited to either endurance type activities or explosive moves. Individuals with a higher proportion of slow or fast twitch fibres are most successful at different activities and the muscle composition *is most likely related to genetic factors supplemented through appropriate exercise training.*[14]

Whilst your dancer sits in that long-winded preparation, not only do the muscles get fatigued and cannot work at their full power and potential, but more riskily, the dancer has time to think and ultimately psych themselves out! I've seen time and time again, especially in a Pirouette Surgery® class, whilst dancers are preparing for the 'big turn', the quad or the five, they dégagé and get to jazz fourth, prepping themselves for the big finish, looking around, breathing, moving the arms here and there, and whilst all this happens, that jazz fourth is getting fatigued.

On closer inspection of our industry's 'good multiple turners', they use that plié at the very last second to snap up to retiré and find the force for the turn.

---

14   Bushman, Barbara A. *ACSM's Resources For The Personal Trainer*. 4th ed. Lippincott Williams & Wilkins, 2014. Print.

Advice from the Pirouette Doctor:
(A little girl once called me that... I like it!)

Example teachers' manual exercise

'Further leg torque'
Level 3

- 1 2 – Dégagé to second
- 3 – Place foot in fourth straight legs
- 4 – Push down into plié
- & – Find retiré position/turn
- 5 6 7 – Hold
- 8 – Recover

Suitable in both parallel and turned out positions.

This is also an exercise option with chassé pas de bourrée, with the same counts for the 'prepare to fourth' and syncopate the relevé from the plié.

Too Fast!

On the other hand, when learning pirouettes and doing just a single or a double, if preparation for the pirouette is too quick, the retiré position and grounding of the turns will suffer. With younger pupils or those new to turning, I would advise not to add the syncopation '4 &' action. In preparatory turning having the ability to be up '5' is a suitable timing. '4 &' gives you power for speed, but very little power, and barely any speed, are needed for just one turn.

Too Narrow!

This is definitely apparent in the younger dancers. A lack of muscle development and understanding of muscle placement, along with young dancers taking everything literally, mean that the preparation jazz fourth often looks more like an acrobat trying to balance on a tightrope than presenting a nice grounded position to inject lots of power into the turns. It also means that the movement up to retiré has very little space to land anywhere other than perfect without a topple.

Knees knocking and arms floundering to maintain balance in the preparation doesn't constitute a stable preparation for turning, we all know that.

It all boils down to muscle memory and practice, as well as proprioception development, which comes with age. However, the younger dancer who is working towards turns must have their preparation in the correct place and practise it there indefinitely; otherwise it will hinder their development. Whilst a rickety double might happen with sheer force if all the other positioning is correct, the hope of ever pushing multiples from this narrow position is pretty low.

I like to tell them a train needs to fit through their feet; it's a double-decker train too, so there must be a space between the knees.

Working on a wooden floor also helps if they imagine they have one foot on one plank, a plank between the middle and the other foot on another plank.

Too Wide!

Movement of COG to axis for wide preparation.

In contrast, a preparation that is too wide also hinders a turn.

Jazz fourth is the preparation that we most often go to when we prepare for pirouettes. Stylistically a jazz fourth should be low and long and deep. Often we hear these called 'fat fourths!' (I assume these days that this statement is politically incorrect!)

Unfortunately a 'fat fourth' isn't going to be optimum to turn from either. If you observe the arrows. This is the movement of her centre of gravity (COG). We want to create a preparation position that causes the COG the least movement. By having a fourth too wide the centre of gravity does not just have to go upwards, but also make a substantial movement into the centre of the body and also forward. Often too much weight is placed on the back foot and then the transference again is bigger than it needs to be, therefore adding a further qualm to the consistency and successes of the turn.

Ah... Just Right!

The perfect preparation will be different for everyone. It all depends on the placement of the centre of gravity as well as the strength in the core and legs. Everyone's bodies are different but there are guidelines that can help create the most effective position for everyone. This is the preparation position that Sophia Lucia uses and advises.

How to get your perfect preparation (Jazz Parallel Pirouette)

Step 1 – Stand with your feet in parallel. Feet should be hip distance apart.

Step 2 – Dégagé your leg back straight with the demi-pointe still on the floor without moving the hips. Both legs should still be straight, and hips and shoulders not twisted.

Step 3 – Bend both knees slightly, focusing three quarters of the weight on the front foot and just a quarter on the back demi-pointe. The back demi-pointe should be on its highest arch, pushing the arch forward.

Sophia Lucia demonstrating optimum turning preparation

Step 4 – As you want to pirouette, increase the plié, pushing weight into the front heel and push up on to demi-pointe quickly.

Why this works

I have seen this change a dancer's pirouette tenfold.

- By keeping the weight on the front foot, the centre of gravity only has to go up to the relevé. It doesn't have to move forward or sideways.
- Keeping the leg in hip-width alignment allows the knee to just move forward and eradicates any extra movement or confused placement.
- Pushing off a forced arch position helps, not only the power, but also allows the pelvis to stay in neutral alignment, which is advantageous to the placement of the torso in the turn.

An object's centre of gravity must be directly above the point of contact with the floor for it to balance.

Initial Reaction Phase (Timing and Transition)

With all preparations for dance movements, the entire body needs to be engaged and ready to fire quickly. This comes from dynamic barre work and drill exercises. It is important that the arms and retiré action happen as one and there is no supporting foot anticipation. By moving the foot momentarily before the body, it opens the working hip and shoulder and the arms drag behind the body. The leg pulling up the retiré position is a critical instant phase and one that must be focused on. Slow, sloppy drawing to retiré in preparatory turning exercises will only lead to a weak start to turning training.

Strong ankles also play a big role in this critical initial reaction. We discussed this further in the section 'Spaghetti Legs'.

The hardest part in turns for young dancers is the movement of the leg up into retiré from the preparation. It is important that they don't wait too long to get to that optimum 'airtight' position. It's therefore good practice to accent your counts as a teacher. Instead of 'Prep 1, lift leg to retiré, 2...', use 'Prep 1, snatch, &...'.

Arms for Preparation

There is more focus on the arm position in the section dedicated to the *Tyrannosaurus rex*.

Arms in preparation, again, differ for everyone and this is also down to stylistic preference.

If we were to take a jazz pirouette, the arms that I recommend would start in opposition jazz third (balletic third position straightened). An important thing to remember is that in ballet the side arm is always in front of the torso and not behind it, the same should be apparent in the arm preparation for turns. Especially in smaller numbered rotations, there doesn't need to be any wind up of the arm and keeping the gap between the arms smaller helps the torso and core muscles connected to the arms make a more defined and optimum tension. If the arm is behind the position 'whip' is found and this often pushes dancers off balance.

The other arm is directly forward and at shoulder height, with the lats pulling down.

There are two options then for the arms to close in.

Option 1 - involves the side arm moving to join the front arm directly in front of the body without the front arm moving towards the side. This creates a great connection in the core and trains excellent muscle memory for how the arms need to be.

Option 2 - involves the front arm moving towards the direction of turn, often moving to á la seconde, and the arms coming together in en avant at about a quarter of the way around. This allows the turn to start with a larger moment of inertia and could help stabilise the balance. The downside to this is that it could also knock inexperienced dancers off balance. These dancers often have less body control and less isolated muscle tension, therefore if you say move your arm to the side and let the other one join it, it soon becomes a whipping and spinning movement.

Developing the use of the arms, as long as the starting position and turning position are using dynamic muscle tension, is a personal choice.

I got my husband to demonstrate these two options. As a trained dancer, he admitted that his body had got into the habit of doing option 2, but when he tried option 1 he said his body felt more controlled and he could exert more power at the start of the turn.

Once more turns are required, I'm talking six plus at least, the front arm placement needs to change to gain further momentum. Notice I didn't say the side arm as well. Even the world's greatest turners do not twist from the spine but instead increase the force by shortening the distance between their two arms; they find the torque in their core as opposed to their body twist. By stepping into a turn and twisting the torso, further strength is required to enable the force from the body to straighten up and, often unless the dancer has a core of steel (which some little dancers these days do have!), increases the topple factor from the turns. 'Campbell Technique' (see arms section) also helps define and increase the number of turns, by increasing the moment of inertia.

Definite 'No-Nos' with the arms

- Loose floppy arms.
- Arms that tilt downwards from the shoulder girdle.
- Droopy elbows.
- Arms that move before the body has even relevéd. (Oh I've seen it.)
- Arms that never connect in en avant and could fit five beach balls between them.

The list could go on... and does go on, in a later section!

The Little Toe and the Ice Skater

The ability to turn relies on force and lack of friction. The ability to increase the force has been discussed with finding torque in the preparation. Friction on the other hand is heavily dependent on what the dancer has on their feet.

A bare foot is an optimum modern dancer's tool and, when demonstrating travelling movements and choreography, allows an elongated line and great connection to the ground. However, bare feet are not optimum for allowing less friction, and in turn, don't enable more rotations. Dancers these days are very lucky that they have a selection of footwear purposely designed to lessen the friction on the floor to perform more turns. Whilst I know some teachers demand that their dancers harden their feet and dance barefoot, the possibility of going around more than four times in a bare foot is very low. Skin and dance floors create resistance and then the friction causes the turn to slow down.

I always recommend turning shoes. These are half shoes that cover the front half of the foot giving complete coverage of the ball of the foot and toes, allowing less friction and ultimately more consistent turns. If these fit properly, then you can hardly tell they are on the dancers, especially the canvas, tan variety. The other alternative is the foot thongs that go between the toes and add a suede turning area to the ball of the foot. Whilst these have a similar concept to the turning shoe, I find that they don't aid turning, mainly due to the fact that the toes are still in contact with the floor and that the little toe always seems to get left behind when turning, especially if you have stubby ones like me, and worst of all, this is terribly painful. I used to wear these at college and by the end of the second year I went to the chiropodist because my little toes were purple! The diagnosis was that they had been fractured and broken so many times from twisting in pirouettes that they were traumatised!

As a contemporary dancer, I have spent a lot of my career dancing in socks. This isn't of course optimum for young dancers because of the slip factor and health and safety however, I had a little student with the above-mentioned thongs. Everything that she did in preparation and balance highlighted to me that she should be able to turn well, but every time she tried it, the single turn was rather inconsistent and after a while she told me her toes were hurting. After around six weeks of training this wasn't getting any better, and for me this was cause for concern (I'm impatient and I've seen my techniques work many times before), so I had her for a private lesson and asked her to bring some socks. Straight away the child did a double turn and is now working on triples. Giving young dancers the best conditions to learn in is so important to their development. I agree that older dancers should toughen up their feet by dancing bare foot, but I don't see that toughening a six-year-old's feet is particularly imperative to their dance development!

In addition to helping dancers reduce their friction for more turns, the correct footwear also can add further force to a turn. Often we see young dancers turning in one sock, or one turner, or one tap shoe. This isn't for fashion but so that they can create more force from the preparation foot that isn't wearing the friction-reducing device! A bare foot and a sock will definitely give the dancers a chance to gain at least one more rotation; this diminishes the slip factor on the preparation torque but keeps the friction low on the supporting leg.
(Also useful if Harlem the Jackapoo has stolen one of your turners!)

If we reduce the friction even more than a sock on a slippy floor, we can begin to relate to ice skaters and the lack of friction that they have when they turn with blades on ice. I was lucky enough to gain an insight into how ice skaters develop their turning technique by speaking to Lulu Alexandra, champion ice skater. The full interview can be found in 'Let's Talk Turns', but I will make one evaluation from it here. Ice-skating is another sport where they begin turning training whilst the children still have no front teeth... I think somehow dance teaching has missed the boat by not practising turning drills before teenage years!

Wait... this is all good, but my dancers are still turning the wrong way!
OK, so far this book has related to turns by dancers who already know what to do, which way to turn and what they're aiming for! However if you are faced with a class of students who are brand new, they will not know what they're meant to be doing and getting them to squeeze their latissimus dorsi is going to be rather pointless. I'm imagining (hoping)

that with this class of students you have demonstrated what you're after, or got someone to demonstrate for you, related your teaching methods to the rest of this book and possibly bought my teachers' manual and are making your way through the level 1 exercises, yet still are struggling to get your dancers to turn the right way!

The only problem with dancers finding their 'spin' is that naturally children will turn inwards. Even once you've taught a dancer how to spin en dehors, the odd en dedans one will still slip in whilst they are young. Trying to get a young dancer to do what you are doing, and time and time again watching them turn the wrong way, is infuriating. I often relate turning to moving when upside down, they don't actually realise or see that they are doing anything different and even when you say go one way, they go the opposite!

I have an exercise for this, which takes the exasperation away! The 'Thumb Slap Exercise'! (Part of Level 1 in the teaching manual.)

This always gets an 'ooh' from teachers who observe my classes!

1. Start with your little dancer (or your big dancer if you've still got the same problem), in their jazz fourth preparation position with the right foot behind.
2. Get them to have their arms in their opposition jazz third position with their right arm in front.
3. Instruct your dancers to do a thumb hitch-hiking action with their right arm in the right direction.
4. Then use the same arm and do a slapping action (not too hard) on the right leg, which is behind.
5. Then tell them that they are going to turn the way they did the thumb and lift the leg they slapped… and hey presto!

Works every time… well maybe 98% of the time!

The other tool I often go to for this problem is the 'magic scrunchie', or once it became the 'pirouette bracelet!' (Thanks to drama lessons as a child and a father who can make anything out of anything, my improvisational teaching strategies are quite imaginative!)

Little children need a visual. So if they're adamantly turning on the wrong leg, and cannot differentiate between this and what they're meant to do, they need something else to give them a nudge! The magic scrunchie/pirouette bracelet (it could even be a pirouette Band-Aid as long as they're not allergic), gets placed around the ankle of the supporting leg and by indefinable magic, the scrunchie makes that leg stay on the ground. It just cannot come off the floor!

Are You a Lean Backer or a Face Planter?
Posture and Core Control

The largest column on the graph, as to why dancers that I researched think that their turns go wrong, was that they 'lose balance'. I actually don't think this is purely down to balance itself; I discussed the science of this in the chapter at the start. I think dancers choose to say they lose balance because they fall off of their turn, which is usually down to their posture and core control.

We do have inner systems that help our balance, the vestibular system mainly, which I discuss in Wheeeeeeeeee Facto section. Sometimes though, talking to your students about the inner workings of their anatomy leads to absolutely no improvement in the actual production of the turn. Similar to the fact that I know the mechanics behind doing a back-flick but I can't actually demonstrate it... any more!

Any stress, fear or tension are complete turn killers. These factors are often linked to the head and I talk about the use of the head a lot in the sections of this book, the importance of placement due to it being the heaviest part of the body and it having the ability to throw dancers off in any direction when not used correctly.

However, sometimes the dancer's head is in a good alignment but it is the upper back and top part of the spine that makes the turns spin off in an unwanted direction. When the spine is in alignment it creates a central point of balance all the way down the body that allows the weight to be evenly distributed for minimal stress on the spine, and in a turner's case, allows their axis to be stable.

Teenage girls come into dance class with sublime posture... can you sense my sarcasm? There is something apparently fashionable about standing with one's hips pushed forward, knees locked back and upper body slumped. I call this the Instagram pose! I have a great deal of problems with my posture, not because I want to stand like this to be cool, but I have a terribly long back which needs extra attention and strengthening to maintain good posture. Why teens like to stand like this beats me, other than perhaps they are tired? Or spend too much time sitting at desks, computers or on their phones at school? However, when these dancers then begin to start turning, good posture locks into place, and as their body isn't used to it, sometimes it counteracts the corrections of the turns and goes too far. Slumped postures stretch the back muscles, so it is important to continue upper back exercises. A range of these can be found in the *T. rex* section.

Dancers that fall off their turns due to posture, in my eyes, fall into two categories; falling either forward or backward.

<u>The Lean Backers</u> – These are students who are so adamantly trying to pull up that they stress the neck area, therefore sending their head behind its correct alignment. Often these dancers are dancers who are dancing with their arms completely bent in a jazz first position and not engaging any parts of their back muscles or arms. As well as lifting up and leaning back due to the weight placement of the neck, the misplaced upper spine means that the pelvis tilts out of neutral and core tension begins to waver. Physically 'Lean backers' frequently have larger bosoms.

How to help

Once the neck and head are in the correct alignment (see 'Spotting' for further pointers), I then stand behind the dancers with a yoga block. The part of the back that they usually throw back is in between the shoulder blades, often because

Block sensory correction

scapula control is weak. I push the block into their back so that they can locate the area of problem with a touch sense, as opposed to just processing the correction mentally. I then stand behind them, far enough away not to put them off, still with the block at the height that they want to think about not throwing backwards from. The subconscious, mixed with the memory of the block being pushed into their back, helps to realign their spine and in time they stop leaning back, although after a growth spurt this always comes flooding back.

This technique is apparent in one of my 'famous' Instagram videos. It demonstrates the block-in-the-back action, as well as showing how dancers should stay up at the end of their turns. Lauren demonstrates five beautiful turns with a perfect alignment. Shameless promotion here… go follow me, @rosiniballerini. (Awkward name, I know! It was my nickname at college before I thought I'd ever have a following. I was going to change it but then Sophia Lucia followed and tagged me. At that point I was in too deep into Instagram to change it! And a big shout out to Edinburgh Dance Academy juniors who created my 'Rosini Ballerini' theme song!)

The Face Planters – This is when the dancers fall forward. Usually these dancers have low and elongated first position arms, nearer to their retiré knee than their sternum. They often contract their abdominals too much and therefore their lumbar spine rounds and their bottom tucks under. This has a knock-on effect and the whole spine rounds, ending with the head being forward of its correct alignment. The 'Face planters' sometimes have tighter hamstrings which tucks their pelvis' under and rounds their spines.

Infamous Instagram video

How to help

Bring out Miley Cyrus. We have her to thank for the crazy twerking phase, but just getting your dancers to stick their bottoms out slightly should then realign their spines; that is if they were contracted in the first place. By neutralising the pelvis the abdominals can work well, but not too much. Asking the dancers to bring their arms in much closer to their bodies will also make a massive difference to these turners.

There are then the dancers that fall sideways, this mainly accentuated by weak preparation positions and unlevel hips. Then there are the children that randomly fall to the floor after finishing quite a nice turn... there's not much science behind that fall... I call those attention seekers! #Burn

Torso Positioning and the Importance of the Core

The core is the centre of the body and connects everything together.

Many think this is just the abdominals but in fact the core is a collaboration of everything from the top of the sternum down to below the groin.

These muscles can act as an isometric or dynamic stabiliser for movement, transfer force from one limb to the other, or initiate movement itself.

If we say squeeze to young dancers, when referring to using their abdominals, it's a very static, often breath-held action. They're never really feeling their pelvic floor in this squeeze and therefore, because the transversus abdominis connect to the hip flexor, which connect the adductors, glutes and hamstrings (do you see where I'm going with this!), their pirouette position isn't going to be the best it can be. I have seen dancers improve from three to five turns just thinking about their abdominals going 'in and up'. Combine that with strong isolated transversus abdominis training, aka Pilates, and tada, a competent more consistent turner is born. I suppose the whole of this book could be consolidated into that last paragraph... but that wouldn't have been so fun!

Imagine your core like a box. The foundation of the core is the pelvic floor. The top of the core is the diaphragm. In the front it's the transverse abs, internal and external obliques, and rectus abdominis. In the back it's the erector spinae muscles and multifidus. (The latter sounds much like a Harry Potter spell!)

Dancers must develop a strong core to prevent injury from increased flexibility, but foremost, to be able to perform complex movements with power. When the core works seamlessly alongside the rest of the body and torques, the movements become easier and more consistent. Alternatively, using the core incorrectly can hinder dancers and cause inconsistency and injury. Many dancers perform lots of crunches in the hope that this alone will strengthen their core, but there is much more to core stability than that.

True Core Stability Is...

- The ability to control the spine dynamically.
- Fine coordination of all of the muscles that control your trunk, not just the abdominals.
- The ability to adjust the level of control needed, depending on the situation.
- Creating a stable base off of which to work the limbs.
- Stabilising the midsection to allow smooth and effective transfer of force through the body.

A dancer's core stability needs to be a well-tuned coordination of all of the muscles, to allow controlled movements without tensing and without holding their breath in one spot.

It is important, especially for turns, that the core moves as one piece and dynamic tension throughout all the areas of the torso contribute to successful turns.

Worst of all with young dancers is that they do sit-ups incorrectly and allow their abdominals to dome. This isn't isolating the correct muscles, but can also cause injury in the lower spine. By doming they are separating the muscles of the transverse abdominis and the rectus abdominis, similar to what happens during pregnancy. We must remember that a flat stomach shows more core control than an over-ripped six-pack. Another major disadvantage of massive abdominal strengthening is that overactive upper abdominals pull the upper body forward, in front of the line of gravity. This creates a stooped posture and the one of a bodybuilder, hardly what we are looking for in our pretty lyrical ten-year-olds.

Breathing whilst drilling abdominal exercises is highly important. You should exhale as you're exerting yourself and inhale when you're ending the exertion and unclenching your muscles. When performing sit-ups and crunches, inhale before your first lift then exhale as you raise your torso. Inhale as you lower your torso back to the ground.

Breathing is massively important to keep the intra-abdominal pressure safe and balanced. Failure to keep this balanced can seriously damage organs and strain internal muscles.

Pelvic Floor Muscles

Kids need to know where their core comes from. The British modesty and stiff upper lip post 10 years old must disperse, so that your dancers can understand how important the 'in and up' action is. Without that how can we expect dancers to demonstrate these difficult moves that need total body connection?

I am sure that many teachers reading this, like myself, are rather reserved and strait-laced when it comes to talking to our students about the workings of their pelvic floor muscles. Whilst the subject isn't taboo, trying to get your eight-year-olds to understand the concept isn't the easiest of tasks without incessant giggling or inappropriate comments, but it is one that needs focusing on because without the pelvic floor engaged the 'box' of the abdominals does not have a bottom! My senior students and I came up with this imagery and it's been my 'go-to' ever since then. We call 'that' area a department store and the pelvic floor muscles are an elevator. That elevator is right in the middle. Now there's no point the elevator going right to the top because that is the staff quarters and there is nothing to buy there (also contracting any abdominal muscle to its extremes isn't dynamic), so instead they go three quarters of the way up to the café on level 6. If you ever see me telling students to take their 'elevators to level 6', now you will know what I mean!

How to train your dancers cores safely and effectively!

Stomach Flattening Exercise

It's good to focus on the breathing method below before doing any abdominal work.

- Lie the children on their backs, with their legs bent, feet on the floor, hip distance apart with parallel feet.
- Get them to interlace their hands behind their heads.
- Instruct them to lift their head an inch off of the floor then push the head into the hands so that their arms act as a neck brace. Their necks then should be completely relaxed.
- From there they should inhale through the nose, expand the chest, then as they exhale pull their belly button into the spine and lock that in, like a popper on a jacket. This is the abdominal brace, which is the starting set-up for all abdominal exercises. Keeping that belly button pulled in, they should then breath in and out without doming.

Until they've mastered the breathing techniques they shouldn't move on to the crunches.

Wrinkle your Sellotape (or any other tape brand available!)

I do not have an obsession with Sellotape... I promise.

This is a particularly good image for little children, who don't know how to engage their abdominals. We say 'squeeze your tummy' and they hold their breath, lift their shoulders up and their ribs open further than ribs should ever open.

I am not sure if this is classed as imagery, but it is an image you can use after the first time you've explained it to your students. The Sellotape is out again. *Just picked up the book and opened it at this page? Head to 'The Sellotape Phenomenon' to find out more!* This time I tape two vertical lines, parallel to each other, from the bottom of the ribs on either side down to the hip bones. Now it's really important that this tape is smooth! Actually, clear Sellotape is ideal for this! (I'm wondering to myself if a more apt title for this book would have been: 'Dance Teaching – Sellotape and I'.) I then instruct the children to try and wrinkle their Sellotape without moving their head, shoulders or bottom, just using their tummy! After you've done this, wow, the improvement in correct abdominal usage is amazing! And guess what? The improvement in the pirouette is amazing too! Teaching dancers to use their bodies properly from a young age is so rewarding in later dance life – less injuries, more consistency and muscular balance.

Correct abdominal usage using tape.

The Crunch

Exhale and lift the shoulders off the floor, flexing the trunk 25 degrees. The thoracic spine is still on the floor. The lumbar spine is neutral and not pushing into the floor. Eyeline is above the knees and the ribs are sliding down to the hips. Draw the belly in. Reset.

In total I would like to see about eight correct sit-ups from children under ten years old.

Maximum necessary to engage the core is 30 - 40 sit-ups.

Variations

- Lifting the heels off, which tucks the pelvis in, to help engage the core more.
- Single knee folds or double knee fold. Tabletop position.
- Oblique crunches – keep the elbows wide and rocking on the shoulders, peel the opposite shoulder off the floor.

Any abdominal exercises that put pressure on the lower back and spine, when the legs are extended out for example, are not safe exercises for children. Until the children have control of the lower torso and pelvis, the legs should be near the body.

Plank

Plank is good if done correctly. Plank can be very unpleasant when done badly!

The plank is one of the best exercises for core conditioning but it also works your glutes and hamstrings, supports proper posture and improves balance. However, practising a plank for a long period of time usually exposes bad form, which is detrimental to improvement, injury causing and uncomfortable. Holding a static posture for long periods of time teaches the body to be stiff and is counterproductive to the dynamic posture a pirouette needs. Moving through plank positions and keeping the body moving is much more beneficial.

Little People in Plank!

Starting on all fours, we walk the hands forward on to the elbows to half plank. The spine should be flat with the shoulders back and down. The head must be in line and lengthened; eyes to the hands.

Hold for 10 - 15 seconds maximum.

Observation:
Gymnasts round their shoulders in plank positions due to the practice of 'dish' for safe tumbles.

(Dish is a strengthening exercise for the core, where the participant has to hold their body in a rigid state. Lying on their back, the legs are lifted slightly off the floor and arms raised above the head. The spine is mainly on the floor but the shoulders and head are lifted. The pelvis is tucked under. This is a great strength exercise but not an optimum training exercise for young dancers' posture, due to the rounding of the spine and tilting of the pelvis. It is instead fantastic for tumbling and acrobatic training and can save the spine if something goes wrong.)

Seniors in Plank

Shoulders, hips and legs should all be in line. Legs should be together and squeezed, with the hips slightly tucked under so it relieves pressure on the lower back. Shoulders must be pressed back and down and the chest is lifted. There is a two-finger squeeze in the shoulder blades to prevent any rounding.

Hold for Thirty seconds to a minute.

Why Not Plank for Ten Minutes?

In real life this isn't practical. Even a short time is enough to stress the body to increase strength in the muscles. In a long time the body fatigues and the positioning will weaken and strength gain in the correct places will be compromised.

Good form is better than long repetitions.

Holding a plank for five or ten minutes, while very impressive, isn't necessarily going to have increasingly beneficial returns. Instead, it's better to add some sort of dynamic movement, such as the body saw. (Don't go forward and back because it causes shoulder impingement but instead back and forward.)

Side Plank

Side plank

Side plank is more beneficial for dancers than normal plank. It connects your whole side body together, the latissimus dorsi, obliques and glutes – really important muscles in turns.

Elbows must be underneath the shoulder. Feet are stacked or can be crossed. Lift the hips as high as you can so the calves come off the floor. For weaker dancers, the regression is that the underneath leg is bent and supporting, and the top leg is off of the floor.

Hold side plank for 30 seconds to a minute.

Variations

- Hip lifts. Moving the hips up an inch and back.
- Threading the needle. Where the top hand reaches around through and under the plank and touches the supporting shoulder as the chest comes forward and then opens back out.

For advanced students – You can lift the top leg to retiré position and sequence turning out and in.

Roll Downs with Resistance Bands

Abdominal roll down with resistance support

Especially for younger dancers these are great. They highlight where the abdominals are. They are particularly safe because they are supported by a band and the pressure is off the hip flexors.

The band is placed around the feet and beside the thighs, held with a light tension. Sit up tall and start to roll down through the spine all the way down, using the band as a guide and not pulling on it. As they roll back up, pull the chin to the chest and up through the vertebrae, always going in a C curve, with the pelvis tucking under the spine rather than a straight line, just like you do when you roll down through the spine when standing up.

How Can Gyrotonics® and Gyrokinesis® Principles Help Turns?

In the fitness form developed originally as yoga for dancers, Gyrotonics® uses specialised equipment that permits one to move with support and resistance. The theory is that movements have five lines; left to right, up and down and then the fifth line. The fifth line extends through the bone marrow of the body parts. With that image instruction in mind, take your arms firstly to á la seconde. Do you feel the difference in strength and stabilisation once the fifth line is involved? Now imagine that with all the body parts connected with the pirouette position. Yes, you feel it! Getting your students to feel that won't be so easy, yet when they do their turns will become stronger because their position is supported better.

The Wheeeeeeeeee Factor

Finding Your Spin

There are those children who just won't turn. Fear floods their expression. No sooner have they lifted the foot off the floor and it's back down again! It's highly likely these are not young children but most likely the teenager who has never experienced turning when they are younger. They are now 14 and freaking out, and possibly lacking any 'wheeeeeeeeee' factor, which is surprisingly easier to find than the X factor!

Who remembers the joy of the school Christmas disco, before health and safety regulations killed the fun? The pure exhilaration of seeing that freshly buffed and very shiny wooden floor, knowing full well that within an hour your glittery kitten heels would be off and you'd have the chance to slip, slide and spin to your heart's content. Well, until someone slipped a little too hard and there were tears, although everyone was back up spinning in five minutes. It's highly unlikely that these children I describe at the party are also 14 and *freaking out*, they're more likely to be four or five-year-olds loving life! The age that I feel it is appropriate to start turning classes. Remember, my research findings draw attention to the fact that most UK dancers start pirouette training when they are 13... Yet Sophia Lucia started at four. I'm sure you see a pattern forming!

Children like to spin and they ultimately do it with no fear, which is because they are in an unknown field, unaware of the danger and are learning to test their balance. Movements such as spinning, rolling and hanging upside down, the things that all kids like to do, are stimulating their vestibular system and establishing their sense of balance. By spinning, young children are testing what it feels like to be in and out of balance. Children with a highly developed vestibular system are very happy to turn, jump, roll, or hang upside down and they are quite relaxed knowing their body will adapt to the movement created; this is known as gravitational security. However, this is the first sensory system to fully develop, so it is important to begin turning processes in younger classes. The balance system is under construction until around 13 or 14 years of age, subsequently it seems slightly pointless to start teaching pirouettes then like dance exam boards recommend!

Now, let's picture the local fairground, children and pre-teens on the carousels, having a lovely old time. The older we get the less we seem to enjoy the motion! I remember loving the rides as a child, and then I went to the local fair when I was around 19 and got the most severe motion sickness! I was home in bed within an hour! With the exception of circus performers, for the most part, our desire to spin dwindles out after childhood.

Scientists are not sure why this is, even though there have been a lot of studies over time. There are many theories, all of which have rather scientific names, such as intravestibular conflict... but I said this book wouldn't get too scientific!
The brain nevertheless is a very amazing organ and it can learn to compensate when balance is lost, whether it be through infection or aging. There are also specific exercises that can improve reactions to dizziness.

Lucy Yardley is a professor of health psychology at the University of Southampton. She says that 'there might be an aspect of 'use it or lose it', in the decrease of tolerance with dizziness with age. Older people's balance systems would benefit from spinning too'.

It is not a lost cause if we have a dancer who is a late starter, however, if we are looking for consistency, lack of fear and the production of more turns, it seems developing our spinning sensation whilst younger is imperative.

Now, back to the point and how this will help your dancers in class.

Even though it takes time for reserved teenagers to let go, getting your whole class to make a 'wheeeeeeeeeee' sound as they turn will eradicate too much fear, and ultimately a double turn will come without trying, albeit in a funny position! It's important to feel the sensation of spinning and then use it as a catalyst for the pirouette action, especially for more turns.

TurnBoards are another tool to aid this spinning feeling. Professionals have mixed opinions on these boards, due to incorrect weight placements, lack of need to prepare and danger, however there are many plus points to them too. It is not my place to endorse or disfavour these, it is up to you to make your own decisions!

I do have a case study observation for TurnBoards though. I have taught one little girl to turn since she was five years old (for just 30 minutes a week). At seven she could do perfect double turns. Then for Christmas along came a TurnBoard. Suddenly, out of nowhere, her beautiful turns disappeared. She became so frustrated and then blurted out, 'But I can do so many on my TurnBoard'. I had noticed her weight placement changing but thought it was due to growth, as I didn't realise she practised that often with a board. I banned the TurnBoard for a couple of weeks and took her back to her practice basics. The double, and now triples, are back. I always say, 'if you practise for ten minutes a day, one minute practise on the board for the spin, nine minutes without'.

One tool that I like to use to help find the sensation of that extra turn is the gliding disc, often used in gyms for core exercises. Alongside proper technique, feeling the vibe of the turn is one of the most important factors for pirouette success.

Now, as long as it isn't parental watching week, go and instil some wheeeeeeeeeee factor in your classes. Who prefers it; your tiny tots or your adult tappers?

Rhythm

The rhythm of the turn is what many professionals mention as the most important thing to keep turns successful and consistent. Although if we are honest, as dance teachers, the rhythm is the last thing that we teach and that's if we remember to mention it at all. Whilst we teach and know the timing of the pirouette, especially with syllabus turning exercises that fit the music or the specific count, is this the rhythm of the turn? Our focus when teaching turns is unmistakably on the other hundreds of technical elements.

When working with dancers in Pirouette Surgery® workshops, adding my rhythm techniques is often one of the most lucrative teaching points to improving their turns. Using the rhythm of the head at the start and end of the turn actually instils spotting without realising it.

Once a child has the ability to hold even just one turn in the correct positioning, finding the rhythm, I feel, should be the next step. This is even before we begin spotting, as this habitually begins, albeit sometimes after a long, long while, once the rhythms have been established. If a dancer is still struggling with spotting after two or three years of turn practice, teaching tips on spotting can be found in the next section.

Fun Fact! - *From Bailey Callahan, Radio City Rockette*

How do you get your turns all in sync with each other?

> *We all do our choreography on the in-between counts. So, from our preparation, to our spots, to the finish, each is on the 'and' or 'a' count. So that's how specific we get with our turns, but we don't do more than a triple.*

There are two procedures that I use to instil the rhythm of the turn.

Firstly, **Rhythmic Imagery;** this isn't just the *visualisation* of the turn but bringing together a range of other sensations to craft a really vivid image.

Imagery works so well with all kinds of dancers, young or old, beginner or professional. However, it only works if you develop your imagery to inspire the correct ages and refrain from using boring, used-to-death ideas. 'Picking flowers' for soft hands in baby ballet springs to mind! (Imagery Surgery could be another add on book?)

The Doppler effect is something I often refer to in class, skimming past the science of the changing frequency of the waves and heading straight to making a racing car driving around a racetrack noises. Neeeeeeeooooooooommmm! Neeeeooooooommm! I will always remember my physics teacher at school standing at the front of the class, swinging a ball in some tights around his head, making that sound! At the time, a precocious teenager who didn't want to be told anything, this was just a chance to laugh at him, however strangely enough now, I talk of this scientific idea weekly and it is the only part of my GCSE physics that I remember! By making that sound and also the dancers imagining a racing car around a circuit, it gives the turn a sense of rhythm and also pace. If the dancer imagines the start of the turn as the racing car nearest to them and the highest pitch sound, and then the end of each rotation as the car being the furthest away with a low pitched sound, even if it is a very fast representation of the rhythm of the turn, it does add a pattern to the pirouette. Counting this would perhaps go, with an inflection of the voice, a 1, a 2, a 3. Similarly a siren or a swinging searchlight also would present the same visualisation.

Using breath in the turn too and making 'shwooom' noises also helps!

Secondly, **Adding Physical Timing;** many pirouette techniques include 'thinking about something else' and this can be found throughout my book and pretty much throughout all of my teaching. I like to think of the turn's rhythm differently. Instead of thinking of counting a triple as, '1, 2, 3', I prefer dancers to think, '& 1, 2'. There isn't really any science behind this, except that I've tried it with a range of dancers and it works. Whether it is because they are thinking of something else, whether it be the slight accent and speed change going into the second turn, or just generally not saying the dreaded '3' in their head, setting dancers to think about this really helps the beautiful, smooth revolve of their turns.

This works with any number of turns... '& 1, 2, 3, 4, 5, 6, 7,' although by the eighth turn the dancers have probably stopped counting! Try this out with your dancers when they are practising, the more they do it and the more they feel the consistent rhythm of the turn, the easier constant, successful pirouettes will be!

(I am massively aware that these counts contradict the science behind moment of intertia, and the complete different way around to Cambell technique_ I always say, somethings work for some and other things work for others!)

Breathing

We all know that breathing brings oxygen to the muscles and it is also associated with relaxation. These are probably two things that we don't really pay much attention to when thinking of the fundamentals of drills in dance. We think of it more as something that adds dynamics and breadth to our dancer's style and performance. Many syllabi have breath and release exercises to train dancers to coordinate movements with breath and therefore give them a greater range of dynamics.

If you go and see a contemporary company in performance, or even in rehearsal, you will also notice their inclusion of breath in the movements. This is often due to the fact that the piece has no official timing, but the movements are led by inhales and exhales. Therefore the breathing is creating the rhythm for the dancers.

So when we connect this to pirouettes, the breathing helps by setting a rhythm. Also breathing out allows the dancers to relax and not stress too much. I talk about this in the spotting section regarding relaxed necks and faces.

However there is much more to the importance of breathing than these mere superficial entities.

When we think of the trunk muscles we most often associate these with core stabilisation and posture control, but very rarely with how these interact with breathing. The same muscles that are used to stabilise the trunk are also responsible for breathing. The diaphragm has a very important role in trunk stabilisation as well as respiration. Using it increases intra-abdominal pressure, stiffening the torso and also supporting the spine. The diaphragm's role in breathing will always override its role in posture control, so when breathing is more difficult, posture control decreases. Therefore if we hold our breath, don't use the diaphragm as posture control and its only focus is breathing, our posture will be compromised, leading to an increased risk of falling off balance. The same thing happens when the inspiratory muscles are fatigued; we only have to observe runners at the end of a race to see their postural differences to the start.

It is therefore important to train our dancers to use their muscles with the aid of breathing too. Crunches or fitness exercises without the proper use of breath are counterproductive. Using functional breathing training makes exercises more effective and safer, as well as enhancing performance, because it allows the breathing muscles to accommodate their role in stabilising the body's core.

In a Pilates class members use breath to optimise the muscle contracting, therefore we should include these exercises in dance to improve the efficiency of movements too.

So, whilst breathing is great to create rhythm in a turn, it also has a less superficial importance too.

Ask your dancers to breathe in as they prepare and then exhale as they turn. Obviously for the longer turns, breathing will need to happen naturally in the continued rotations. Some dancers don't even know what their breathing is doing as they turn. The most important part of the turn is that first explosion to relevé, so using the functional breathing there has great advantages. When the start of the turn is successful, it's likely that the rest of the turn has a good chance!

Sound Effects

Another way that breathing helps keep the rhythm is by using it to vocalise a 'swooshing' sound. Sounds cannot be made without air flow. This is a great tool for those dancers that 'spin' rather than turn. By slowing their power and wheeeeeeeeee factor right down, and getting them to do three short exhales evenly as they turn, helps them to feel the momentum as they turn.

Alternatively, humming (loosely or else the neck will tense up) a tune as they turn, or even singing a little song, will help to keep rhythm! Mainly these ideas take their mind elsewhere and eradicate any stress or tension.

Finding the rhythmic stability of a turn makes them look controlled, lacking the 'luck' aspect and therefore avoiding the dancer's fear of pirouettes. The fear is something that needs eradicating young, or it will stagnate!

Spinners vs Turners

There is a fine line! Dancers need some wheeeeeeeeee factor, but at the same time not too much!

With a controlled turn, we should be able to see the clear 'coin flip', front-to-back action of the turn, rather than just an indistinct, gyroscopic spin. It is considerably easier to control a soft, balanced landing from a proper pirouette than trying to stop the uncontrolled momentum of a spin by essentially falling or stumbling to the finish position. I call them enthusiastic bulldozers, children who will give everything they have to improve; less has always been more for me. When I teach contemporary, I want subtlety. When I teach leaps, I want correct placement of power and impetus. When I teach turns, I want even and consistent momentum. Sometimes these dancers are so eager to please that actually they put too much power into their turns and it becomes a mess! Therefore when they start getting frustrated and tell me that 'they just can't do it any more', I ask them to show me the slowest turn they can… Often by bringing it back down to mechanical usage, and not brute force, the turn becomes smooth again. The dancers are then refuelled with 'turn-esteem' and back they go to pushing for further turns, whilst being reminded to do them as slow as possible!

Have You Got More 'Chins' Than a Hong Kong Telephone Directory?

(A really bad joke, courtesy of Roger Andrews.)

Spotting

This whole section is dedicated to the best friend and also worst enemy of pirouettes… spotting! The title will make sense soon.

Dancers use spotting during the execution of turns. Its main purpose is to maintain a steady orientation for the dancer's head and eyes to prevent dizziness. However, it is also very useful when used to maintain the rhythm and keep the direction of the turns, as well as aiding balance. As a dancer turns, spotting is performed by rotating the body and head at different speeds. While the body rotates smoothly at a reasonably constant speed, the head periodically rotates much faster and then stops, so as to fix the dancer's stare on a single 'spot'. Spotting is used in many kinds of turns, except for those tours in adage where a sudden movement of the head would affect the serenity and fluidity of the slower turns.

Spotting is important, however, this is where people begin to disagree with how important it really is. Some dancers say that they do not spot; others swear that without a spotting action there would be no turn at all.

The disagreement lies within the actual description of the spotting action and how different teachers have interpreted it over the years.

Let me explain.

The body uses three systems to establish balance, the proprioceptive system, the visual system and the vestibular system.

The Proprioceptive System

There are sensory receptors located in the body's muscles, tendons and joints that respond to changes in pressure and send messages to the brain letting it know where the different parts of the body are and how they are moving in relation to other body parts.

The Visual System

The visual system helps determine where the body is in space. Within this system is the body's optical righting reflex. This reflex helps ensure that we remain upright by working to keep both eyes on the horizontal plane.

The Vestibular System (More information in *Wheeeeeeeeeee Factor*)

The vestibular system helps the body maintain balance through the anatomy of the inner ear. This system gives the brain information about the body's position during movement. The ear canals are filled with fluid and lined with cilia, or tiny hairs, that are sensitive to the movement of the fluid. When the position of the head shifts during movement, the cilia send signals to the brain to activate the muscles that keep the head vertical.

Whilst pirouettes are being learnt the body cannot totally rely on the proprioceptive system until the turn and its position are in our muscle memory, therefore the other two are relied upon to maintain balance. By focusing on one place, it eradicates the brain becoming confused by processing multiple images. To preserve balance the head must be kept steady and in a level position, this is to manage the dizziness and also prevent the body from trying to save itself. The Healthy Dancer Blog[15] mentions:

When the head tilts too much to one side, the visual system senses the horizontal shift and the vestibular system signals the brain to force the body to right itself. When this occurs, the dancer will either begin to hop to save the turn, or fall out of the turn in an effort to re-establish the body's vertical position in space. It is important that dancers be trained

15   Thehealthydancer.blogspot.co.uk. (2013). *The Healthy Dancer: Spotting & Why It Works.* [online] Available at: http://thehealthydancer.blogspot.co.uk/2013/06/spotting-why-it-works.html [Accessed 28 Jun. 2016].

to simply turn their heads while spotting and to eliminate any tilting motions. Waiting to quickly rotate the head back to the focal point until the last possible moment will also ensure that as little movement occurs as possible. By adding these two concepts to the idea of staring at a focal point, dancers can improve their turning technique immensely.

I believe that spotting has become something that it never was designed to be, hence why sometimes it makes the pirouette worse. Nowhere in the above description does it say move the head so sharply that it gives you whiplash, or tense your neck and thrash it around. It says keep the head vertical, focus on one point and quickly rotate it. Whilst whipping too fast or strong can throw a dancer off balance, moving the head too slowly can disrupt momentum and the turn becomes separated and whirlwind-like.

Your head is the heaviest part of your body and, when used correctly in a turn, it can really help the rotations. When used incorrectly, however, prepare to fall out of every turn you try! Centre of balance and weight placement play a massive role in turns. Imagine a perfectly balanced old-fashioned weighing scale (this is a pirouette position with a well-placed head with optimum neck alignment), now add around four bags of sugar (that's how much your head weighs, 4kg!) on to one side (left, right or front, back). Primary school mathematics explains that the scale will now tip to one side. As will your pirouette!

ABT's Gillian Murphy states, 'Natural rhythm and spotting technique is most helpful, but it is highly unique to each individual dancer.'

I try not to teach spotting. What I try and do is get the dancer to feel the rhythm of their head action and this more often than not turns into an excellent focus and spot action. Using the front and back of the dancer's head, the focus on moving each part helps the action stay even and rhythmical.

There is more information on my imagery for spotting later but my most successful and lucrative technique is this:

Dancers have a crayon on their chin and a torch in their bun. As they turn the crayon draws a line on the wall and then the torch follows by lighting it up. By doing this the children focus on front then back then the front again, creating a good movement in the head when turning. Crayon, torch, crayon, torch... equals a lovely double turn!

Common Mistakes with Spotting

Double Chins

(Now do you see where the section title was coming from?)

'I stress out' was one of the most common responses to my research as to why dancers dislike turns. Not only does the stress alter the mentality and psychology of the turn, but also the tension in the neck. To be able to move your head freely and perform a smooth spot, a stiff neck isn't very useful or very comfortable.

Turtlehead, thumb face or double chins, whatever you want to call it, must be eradicated from the dancer to create a loose spotting movement.

My mum, also a dance teacher (wait, she's more of a dance legend, but that's another story), has always told dancers to stick their tongues out when their pirouettes are going wrong and my Pirouette Surgery® answer to those that have tense necks is based on this. Open your mouth and stick your tongue out, this relaxes your face and your jaw, allowing lots of freedom of movement during the spotting. I often get dancers to try a simple pirouette both ways and the difference is incredible! A similar technique is used in singing to relax facial muscles. Obviously not many performances are going to allow for dancers to turn with zombielike expressions however, it is a really great teaching tool for those struggling with stress. Once the relaxation has happened, putting the tongue away is the next step. Try blowing out loosely as the turn happens, less and less, until the face is just relaxed naturally when performing pirouettes.

If the silly face dissolves your class into hysterics (often the younger dancers) or the other end of the spectrum, your teenage dancers are just too cool for that childishness, the same effect happens if you make them say something as they turn. 'A double pirouette', 'vanilla ice cream', 'Rosina's the best', or whatever floats your boat, works wonders too. You can't really speak well with a double chin... and I bet you all just tried it!

The Epic Stare

This happens regularly with younger dancers. They try so hard to keep focus on that one spot that their head protrudes forwards, resulting in them falling forwards. Younger dancers associate staring with being nosey and therefore their pirouettes don't go up and around, just straight forward!

Teachers often say spotting your head is pointless if you don't focus your eyes on to something, but this is where I disagree. I think that eye focus is imperative for balance, but not for spotting. Feeling the front and sensing the frontal focus consequently allows better spotting motion with very little shift in the neck alignment.

Try and do a pirouette with your eyes closed and allow yourself to feel the front in each rotation. Then try again with your eyes open, not using your eyes to lead you, but instead the whole face feeling the front. The turn feels more natural to most dancers. Alexander Campbell of the Royal Ballet also admitted to me that he isn't a fantastic spotter and it's something he doesn't think about. Moving his head isn't important to him, but feeling the front with his shoulders and torso is.

If the dancers are still falling forward, emphasis on the up action of the head also helps. If they have a high ponytail, hold it (don't pull too hard) and let them turn, imagining they are baubles hanging. Even just standing with your arm in the air above them helps them visualise this.

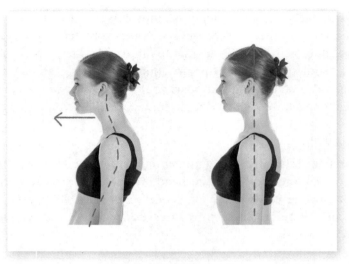

Spine and head placement

I Whip my Hair Back and Forth; I Whip my Hair Back and Forth!

We have American dance competitions to blame, or possibly thank for dancers' extremely high, extremely tight and rather large hair buns. One parent described the hairstyle as looking like her daughter had a 'bread roll on her head'. Then again, a good spotting action is aided by a secure hairstyle, especially in the practice and learning stages. Dancers will never want to move their heads if their plaits are whacking them in the eye, or the loose strands of their ponytail. More tension arrives when a dancer's hairstyle becomes loose and they endeavour to keep it in without really moving their head at all. Maybe you call it old school, but a good solid bun for technical dance classes is never a bad thing! 'But professionals must learn to dance with their hair' I hear some objectors mutter and I totally agree, but your 12-year-old isn't a professional, even if she does have 15,000 followers on Instagram. Let your hair down once your technique is perfect, there are enough things to focus on in pirouette preparation without having to worry about perfect hair!

Whiplash

Moving the head too sharply will result in, most obviously, neck pain and also far too much momentum, as well as a vast difference in the speed of the head in relation to the body! A lot of falling off balance will occur here and very little turning! Also focusing on a really strong spotting action often makes the dancer forget all the other, far more important, things! I like my dancers to have a strong but smooth head movement, with a complete range of motion at the same speed. I call it 'bun torch'; if the dancer's hair is at mid height in a bun, tell them to imagine that a torch is in the middle of it and that the torch must see the whole room evenly, like a disco light, or a searchlight. I mentioned that earlier in my 'crayon, torch' rhythm. I want them to make sure the torch searches the whole room evenly, and not just one side, then the front really fast. Moving the light around the room transforms the focus on spotting from the front and the eyes, to the back of the head and makes a big change, especially for those students who really struggle with moving their head in turns at all. (*Bun torches*, possibly my next entrepreneurial endeavour?)

Sometimes by describing the movement as a whip the dancers tense up again and we're back to sticking that tongue out for relaxation. So, I prefer to use words like, stable, even, direct, secure, firm, level and constant when teaching spotting. A teacher's use of words is very important to impressionable students. Parents might like to remember that too when sending emails… 'Parent Surgery'… probably not a best seller. This is why I absolutely detest hearing teachers yell *whip* whilst dancers are trying to turn. If I started yelling in your face would your neck, face and general energy be positive and relaxed?

The other extreme to this is no movement whatsoever; the dancers enjoy a great panoramic view of the room. Now if the dancer is a natural turner spotting isn't really necessary for the reliability of the turn, but more for the aesthetics of it. It looks nice if the dancer keeps focus on the front. If the dancer isn't a natural turner however this is going to cause quite a bit of a problem to the success of the turns. Firstly observe why the dancer doesn't want to move their head, is it their hair, or perhaps they wear glasses, do they have a neck injury? If it's none of the above, which need to have a slightly more careful approach when teaching turns, ask the dancer to imagine their chin is doing the spotting, a change of focus and something different to using their eyes really helps. Also some dancers need reassurance as to when it is they need to move their heads, so tell them to move their chin when you clap. This takes practice on the teacher's part to get the clap at the right time, but the sounded instruction of the clap instigates the movement.

The Size of the Spot

Children take everything literally. When you say choose a spot on the wall they choose something very, very specific.

I once had a child tell me, when she was working with me on focus, that she was spotting the freckle on my nose…! If you know me, then you'll know I'm not a freckly skin kind of person, so the likelihood was that she was spotting a blackhead! *Children; charming but brutally honest.*

If our chosen focus is too small, too much concentration is used to find the minute detail on the wall and so the turn with the emphasis on well-focused eyes and movement of the head gets lost! The same goes for if they choose something too big, 'the wall'. A paper plate size area is a good shape to find. I made spotting props with those iPhone emoji faces… practical and so #ontrend.

It's also really helpful, especially when working in a group or across the diagonal, that you tell your dancers to spot along and out above the person in front's head. Seeing beyond the dancer in front who could ultimately make them look cross-eyed!

Emoji spots!

Unplanned Changing Spot

I often see dancers who do one, or maybe two, lovely turns with a forward facing spot and then the following turns, with a spot, gets distracted and moves all around the room.

Sometimes this happens in Pirouette Surgery® workshops because they are nervous, or perhaps a parent has just walked in the room and caught their eye. My best advice for this is to place something brightly coloured in front of them where they need to spot, a water bottle, a teddy bear (every dance studio has one of those!), yourself, just so there is something that they must focus on. This, along with the other spotting techniques, makes a massive difference. Conversely, if nothing helps and the focusing on something in front doesn't alter the turn, it might be down to a visual impairment or a learning disability such as dyspraxia, where children struggle with spacing and eye focus. If this is the case, glasses or therapy might be the only option to improve the wandering focus.

Top Tip:

Children are always looking for approval from their teacher so your placement in the room whilst trying to get them to spot is very important. Don't feel the urge to teach them into the mirror by standing behind them, as they will always end up facing you and not back to the front. In a private lesson be directly in front of the dancer and try to get your eyes level, so with smaller dancers kneeling or sitting is advantageous. In a class situation, staying well out of the way is often best and lower down than their spots, so as not to obscure their view. You'll often see me squatting at the front of the class. I like to think I'm Beyoncé but I'm probably just cracking my hips, whilst not obscuring spots.

Spotting Imagery

As with all dance teaching, imagery is one of our most valuable teaching tools. Spotting is no exception! Below I have listed some of my favourite and most successful metaphors for just the head movement, there are many others which I have noted throughout this book.

I am a photographer and I want a photo of your face completely front on.

You are a bauble hanging from the ceiling, nice and loosely hanging.

Your neck is liquid and your chin is floating around on top of it.

Your eyes are lasers; laser a hole through the wall in front of you for as long as you can without lasering a hole through all the other walls!

Training Exercises for Spotting

Some of these can be found in the teacher's Three Level Programme however, there are lots of exercises that can be done separately to help with the head and eye action, as well as making sure the head is always working in a way to optimise the turn.

1. Skipping by half turn from the corner.
2. Walking or running in circles on the spot, facing another child

and having to maintain eye contact for as long as possible. Do this exercise with the body doing a full rotation in four counts and the head doing its rotation on the '& 4' to get the syncopation.

3. The Clock Game (see further on in this chapter)

4. Log Rolling... Dance master David Howard had a very unorthodox way of teaching when I attended his classes in NYC. An amazing old man, but also very old school and passionate, he definitely wouldn't mince his words! Once he exclaimed to someone that they should, 'Try tap dancing, and if that doesn't work, give up!' However, he did have a rather interesting way of teaching spotting, albeit embarrassing if it was you he picked on! When trying to spot we often force the head too much and it really should work in connection to the body for the best results. Before any turning exercise he made some people get down on the floor and log roll. He said it breaks down the fear of turning and also makes them use their whole body at once instead of twisting bit by bit in an awkward way. A fabulous exercise for eight-year-olds, a rather degrading exercise for fully grown adults!

5. Slow motion. Try getting your dancer to do their pirouettes in slow motion, working specifically on eyeline and spotting. Thank you technology for the advancement of phone cameras, their slow motion feature is fantastic for detail and suddenly the kids think you're cool! Well, that all depends on what case you have your phone in; I highly recommend a Victoria's Secret one!

Interesting Fact!

The *Daily Mail* posted an article entitled, 'Why a ballet dancer never gets dizzy: Scientists uncover differences in ballerina's brains that mean they can do endless pirouettes.'[16] Whilst this article is nothing new to us as dancers or teachers it does make some interesting points.

The research used 20 female dancers and 20 female rowers and observed

---

16   Mail Online. (2013). *Why a ballet dancer never gets dizzy: Scientists uncover differences in ballerina's brains that mean they can do endless Pirouettes.* [online] Available at: http://www.dailymail.co.uk/sciencetech/article-2434572/Why-ballet-dancer-gets-dizzy-Scientists-uncover-differences-ballerinas-brains-mean-endless-Pirouettes.html [Accessed 28 Jun. 2016].

their reactions physically, mentally and chemically to spinning. Research found that not only did dancers use their spotting techniques to eradicate dizziness, but also their cerebral cortex is smaller within their vestibular systems. It implies that years of training can enable dancers to suppress signals from the balance organs in the inner ear, which might otherwise make them fall over.

So Close, Yet So Far

The Incomplete Turn

Often your dancer only needs that last little segment to successfully complete the turn. This is down to many things, spotting, psychology, body placement and rhythm, all of which are discussed at length in their main sections.

Multiple pirouettes often look a little messy as, at the last second, the dancers fall from retiré and twist the final part. This is why I find the stopping exercises in my teachers' manual so important. Not only is it important to feel the front with both hips and shoulders (the world-famous and used daily in every dance studio 'headlight analogy'), it's also really important to finish off that extra head.

I often say to my dancers that a double turn involves three heads.

The Static One – the one at the start.

The Middle One – the one finishing the first turn.

The Forgotten One – the one finishing the second turn.

This is obviously added the more turns that you do, triple turns with four heads etc.

Eighty per cent of my researched Pirouette Surgery® participants felt that this made a difference to their execution of further turns because it gave them something to focus on, as well as finding stabilisation in their doubles.

With little ones this is quite a hard complex to grasp and this is where the Clock Game comes into play.

The Clock Game

I use this game with younger children, although seniors quite enjoy it too!

Objectives – To help children's spot and focus.
Understanding that a pirouette stops and doesn't spin.

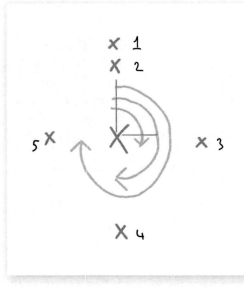

The Clock Game

Players – Dancers need to be in groups of five.

Set-up – Set your children up in a circle, with them placed at quarter past, half past, quarter to and on the hour. If you are aiming for doubles you will need six children and two children behind each other at the o'clock position.

How to play – The aim of the game is that the child gets all the way around the pirouette with good focus and spotting by using the teacher's calls for times and the other children to watch and look at, and hopefully stays up on balance at the end of their named time.

How to win – If the child ends up at the right place they get a point, but if they overshoot they lose a point, perhaps with a little prize at the end; even just a sticker on an achievement chart for the person with the most pirouette clock points.

Advanced level gaming – When aiming for doubles, it is useful to have two dancers at o'clock. Somehow, as soon as you say 'two o'clock', the thought of seeing their first friend bob down to reveal their second friend, makes nearly every little dancer turn around twice!

Staying Up at the End of the Turn

A complete turn in my eyes is one that remains on balance at the end and then the dancer gracefully moves into the position that is desired to move onwards or the aesthetic finishing positions documented through history.

Staying up at the end is beautiful to watch, but often inconsistent, even with some of the greatest dancers. I asked both

Demonstrating a double in The Clock Game

Autumn Miller and Sophia Lucia how they stay up at the end of their turns and neither of them had a specific thought or action that allowed it to happen. Both of them noted that if their positioning whilst turning is solid, and they are 100% on balance, then that is when the turn gracefully runs out of momentum and they just hover in balance.

The stopping must be something that happens in harmony to the velocity and momentum of a turn. It is not something that a dancer can do if there is still 'spin' left in them. The ability to know when the momentum is finishing is something that is only discovered with practice and maturity. My dancers that know how their bodies work and how to engage or relax certain muscles to gain a mechanically optimum movement, are the dancers that can stay up on relevé at the end of a turn before finishing. These are not necessarily the older dancers that I teach, but instead the teenage dancers that I have trained since they were about nine years old with turning drills and have had supplementary conditioning training since that age too.

When a dancer feels that their momentum is dwindling, in order to maintain that balance a further push into the floor from the downward action of the leg, a slight lift of the working leg to re-establish core and glute engagement that may have fatigued during the turn, and a final lock down of the latissimus dorsi, is needed. We should never rush turns to get to the next step. Movement patterns are formed too fast for that! This is why I do not favour too many travelling-turn-training exersises, every time *the prepare then step forward* happens it forms the habit of that being the ending needed.

Keep Turning, Whatever Happens!

At the end of the day, perfecting turning is done by finding the feeling of turning within the body. This is the one place that I find TurnBoards are useful, as it gets dancers' bodies used to the feeling of rotation, one that isn't something that we do every day as normal human beings! Whatever the position, even if both feet are on the floor, keep turning and finish the amount you set out to do! There are 'keep turning' exercises in my Three Level Programme!

It's All in the Mind

With many things, both in the dance world and actually the normal world too, the biggest factor stopping us from doing something isn't physicality but mentality. It often happens in a dance class. A dancer who is usually confident and outgoing becomes tense in the turning section. I touched upon this briefly in the 'Wheeeeeeeeee Factor' section, creating the right psychology and imagery whilst turning is a deal -breaker!

If a dancer is mentally ready and also calm, the pirouette will happen much better than if the dancer is drowned with stress and anxiety! By taking the dancer's mind elsewhere within the turning exercises, even if it is just from the point of view of the teacher using suitably calming words or even their 'yoga voice', a difference will be found.

I use imagery A LOT when I am teaching. I never really noticed until someone pointed this out to me and then I realised every other sentence that comes out of my mouth whilst teaching is imagery based! Imagery works great with little dancers, however it works even better with grown-up dancers. Obviously I pay attention not to patronise students with imagery that isn't age-appropriate, but older dancers can apply the image and the metaphor to their movement quite quickly. Younger dancers take a little bit more time, as they are focused on listening to the 'nice story' instead of applying it to their retirés!

I am a solid believer that when you enjoy something you become good at it. There isn't any way that you can be as good as you physically can be with something that you don't enjoy. It is the same psychology as learning something because you want to, rather than because you have to. Take languages for example, at school I learnt both French and German because we had to. I couldn't see the point in this and I would rather have been in a PE lesson, so therefore I only did the bare minimum in these classes. I think I got a B and an A in GCSE, not too shabby, but still not the best I could have done. I hated languages and therefore I classed myself as not having a linguistic brain. Fast forward ten years: my choreography and teaching have taken me to Italy. I couldn't speak a word when I first arrived and, most upsettingly, I couldn't even order an ice cream in a café! So, when I arrived home I enrolled in Italian classes, dreading them because 'I can't do languages', however when faced with something that I wanted to do, two years later I can speak Italian. Because I want to and because I enjoy it, my improvement in this language is faster than it ever was when learning the other languages for five years! Someone even suggested that I translated this book into Italian; I think I'd need a bit of help with that! Jenny, if you're reading, I'll be calling you! Now, I bet you are thinking, 'Rosina has gone off on a tangent again.' Well what can I say? I am my father's daughter. However, this does all have a point and connects to the mentalities needed to succeed in pirouettes... somehow!

Many of the students that participated in my Pirouette Surgery® questionnaire, in response to stating whether they do or do not like pirouettes and why, said:

'No, I hate them because I just can't do them.'

Take my languages example, or something you've been forced to do. How many times have we said we just 'can't do it', but actually we can? We just needed the correct teaching and tools to succeed. As we were never given those, we automatically jumped to the conclusion that because we can't do it, we never will. Turns are something I want to try and eradicate from dancers' 'I can't' list. This is down to two factors: one, the dancer must want to be able to try and improve their turns, and two (most importantly), teachers must make turns accessible, teach them well over years of progression and also mentally stimulate their dancers in the correct ways when the light at the end of the tunnel seems a little dim.

What are Your Students Thinking?

Whilst imagery in teaching is a major factor for teachers, how a dancer uses their mind will play an important part in the success of their turns and anything else for that matter. On a teachers' intensive I was involved in a life coaching class. I was rather sceptical – I signed up to learn new teaching ideas for my students, not change me, or so I thought. The whole, 'love the world and it will love you back, Instagramable-motivating quote' malarkey isn't something that plays a big role in my life processes. I have a theoretical brain and spiritualism isn't number one. How my perception of positive thinking with dance movements changed after that class!

It is impossible to change anything without changing the state of mind and the older we get the harder it is to change the movement and behavioural patterns we have made.

Therefore if your students' pirouette is not working, in the words of Gina Pero:

'Don't change the pirouette, change the behaviour pattern.'

Dancers that are constantly told 'don't' will see less change than those that are told what to do. That in itself is a behavioural pattern that we as dancer teachers need to change.

Here's an example of this:

'Don't look at the floor when you turn.'
Alters to:
'Look out and connect with your audience whilst you turn.'

Whilst there is much more to turning and improving as dancers than 'positive thinking', I am now converted that it makes a big difference. Maybe I'll even try to apply these principles to my whole life, that's if my analytical and mechanical brain doesn't take over.

I highly recommend checking out specialist, Gina Pero. Her connection to the dance industry, experiences with teachers and coaching experience sets her apart from your average motivational thinker. Perhaps you could book a one-to-one session with her, that would mean going to Las Vegas… but come on, that isn't all that bad!

www.ginapero.com

Imagery examples to Help the Turn and Action

Smoothness

Imagine that your rotations are pearls on a necklace; they are all separate pearls and not a blended together mush of beads. Each turn has its own start and finish, similar to each bead, but they are strung together in a sequence.

This makes the dancers' turns appear rhythmical and lacking that crazy spinning action. It helps dancers demonstrate the start and finish the turns correctly without over spinning, or most regularly observed, under rotating.

Moving your Organs

Sounds a little strange, yet seems to make a difference. Often dancers think of a pirouette (and any dance move for that matter) as a purely extrinsic movement, only using the outside parts of the body. This isn't really a bad thing; ballet class would lose its passion if we were all worried about the bone marrow of our feet doing the tendu movements! However, by thinking of the inside of their body, dancers really use their whole torso. Whether it is that you cannot actually isolate your liver and therefore engage the muscles around it (aka your abdominals… always a positive, whatever the situation!), or that actually telling your dancers to move their organs focuses them on moving the body, especially the torso, in the correct direction… I do not know! Committing one's whole self, spleen included, to the movement definitely helps with the success of any dance move, and in our case turns!

Asking the dancer to feel solidly three-dimensional in space also replicates this technique.

Candyfloss/Cotton Candy/Fairy Floss (dependent on your nationality!)

(This one belongs to you, Grace.)
Dancers need to imagine they are a candyfloss machine and they must complete the whole turn without changing position (especially in the arms) in order to get enough of the sugar from the edges of the candyfloss machine on to their stick, the machine being their turning space and the stick being their body as an axis. This can relate to the cone imagery that is presented in the earlier section.

Turning with the Back

Imagining that turning happens in the back and that the back includes the pelvis, helps for consistent turns with a stable, organised torso. This is often a good image for dancers that fall forward or backward; for them, imagining the back as the main turning point helps centre it directly over the supporting foot.

Lifted by the Ears not the Head

I think every dancer has been told to lift up. Usually this is by the teacher using the imagery that someone has a piece of your hair, or sometimes your ponytail, and is pulling it directly up to the ceiling. I remember often at college, after getting my bun very slick, the late Frank Freeman decided to take a piece of hair and lift it... leaving a lovely bump in my bun.

Now, I totally get where this image is coming from, however it's not my favourite to get children to lift up. Firstly, I teach a lot of teenagers, who are very passionate about their image and wouldn't let me anywhere near their hair, and secondly, I think it's a little risky, trusting your balance on just one lifting point.

At my mother's studio, we have aerial hoop classes. The hoop has two ways of hanging: one with just one strap right in the centre and then the other with two straps equally off-centre. The first option allows spinning to happen in any direction, the hoop can tilt and rock as it pleases. The latter makes the hoop more stable as it can only move in one plane.

Do you see where I am going with this? I like to tell my dancers to lift up from their ears (sometimes eyebrows join in too), instead of their head replicating the hoop with two hanging points. I find that this stabilises their balance, mostly due to the correct placement of their head. If you think of lifting your ears up, go on try it, your head pulls back into its optimum alignment, therefore, helping posture, spotting and balance... the list goes on!

One Less Turn

Think of a double pirouette as one turn: imagine the first rotation as a relevé to the front, which sets you up on one leg. From this you can then add as many turns as you require. The only problem with this image for young children is that they'll go up without any turning momentum and then try and turn whilst they're up there!

Lift Up, Push Down and Lego Bricks!
(The most confusing dance statement ever)

When as teachers we say, 'lift up', we don't necessarily mean actually lift your body up; often this is the statement we use to instruct dancers to find space in their torso, engaging their abdominals, except those very literal children that we teach try to lift their whole body. By just doing that in pirouette the connection to the floor is lost, often hopping happens, and the knee bends; all prerequisites for a failed pirouette.

It is probably more important to push down in a pirouette than any other dance movement. I would also say it is more important to push down than to lift up. There are opposing energies in a turn but it is important to get dancers to understand which parts of them are opposing, rather than exclaiming empty postural advice!

Lego bricks are my go-to reference for many dance-related movements.

Imagine that the top part of you is one brick and the bottom part is another. Lego bricks are strong when they are clicked together, yet when they are pushed together they do not bend or shrink in size. If a dancer connects their core in this way, the bottom half is what is pushing up into the bottom of the Lego brick, but at the same time the top half is pushing down into the top part of the same brick. Whilst this pushing and locking action is happening there is no change in the length of the spine and so the dancer's torso uses opposing energies to engage. The same Lego brick action can then be applied to the legs and their counter energies.

Send Power into the Floor
- Think of your pirouette as a downward spiral into the floor.
- The floor is a magnet and the ball of your foot is pulling into it.
- You're in hard mud, wearing football boots, make nice big holes in the mud with your studs.

All three of these will help dancers keep their connection downwards. Often when dancers think of turning they only focus on the up, which often leads to the ribs lifting and the torso losing strength, as well as hopping, because the foot isn't grounded.

There are many other imagery examples throughout this book that I used. There are also a lot in the interviews at the end.

Kicking the Habit!

Regrettably there is no nicotine patch or Pirouettes Anonymous to help dancers change their habits! (Although, sometimes when I teach Pirouette Surgery® classes at full-time colleges the older students do turn it into a pirouette confession class!) We always want to instil good habits, but bad habits are very easy to pick up, yet time consuming and difficult to get rid of!

The best way to kick a habit is not letting it form in the first place!

Stairway to Perfect Pirouettes!

There are differing opinions as to how much practice dancers should do. I went on a course once, which mentioned that children should practise all the time and it doesn't matter what the quality of the practice is. I do see where they're coming from, especially with things such as basic stretching, but this mentality of quantity over quality does not bode well with pirouette practise! This is because habits are so easily formed, especially in the younger child, who is more eager to practise at home than the 16-year-old who's more interested in getting their hair done for prom! Therefore I instil in my children the idea of stairs as a practice tool for pirouettes.

They can practise them as much as they like, however each turn they do must have thought behind it; using the legs to their best ability, working towards the correct arm shape, thinking about posture and spot. Obviously the focus on the elements of the turn will be different for each age. (My objectives for turners at three levels are included in the teachers' manual.) For every turn that they do to their best ability they are able to take a step up the (never-ending, but they don't need to know that) staircase to perfect pirouettes! Every time they mess around, spin for the sake of it, or don't apply their correction they go clattering down to the bottom of the stairs at the very start again!

But When the Habit is Formed...

A dancer's habitual number of turns is the number that the body is used to aiming for. It is highly unlikely, especially in the UK, that the dancer's initial aim was five turns! Take the first time we see turns in a modern syllabus for example – a double turn is required. So, when a dancer starts doing pirouettes, two is the aim and when they reach that double, the one that is set for the exam, that is where the total number of turns remains at and consequently a habit forms of putting the retiré foot down after two rotations.

I often use techniques to help dancers break this habit. We want dancers that are trained to stay up at the end and then have the choreographer's chosen move to come out of it, whether it is jumping the feet together, stepping to the side, chasséing into chaînés, or whatever. We want dancers to become good turners in any situation, as opposed to turning the correct amount needed to pass the exam.

There are three things a dancer can work on to kick the habit of putting the foot down after the allotted amount of turns and start learning to use their body to turn however many times is needed.

The three things that need most attention when 'kicking the habit' are:

- Rhythm
- Physicality
- Psychology

The rhythm we can consult is the '& 1, 2' formula from the previous earlier section.

For physicality we want to change some things throughout the pirouette.

1. *Preparation*

The dancer's preparation needs to be stronger, not necessarily bigger, but instead using bigger power out of the thighs, this will give the dancer more up power and a more controlled torque. To gain more momentum the dancer will also need to pull their foot into retiré faster, just so it has the best chance of staying there throughout more turns.

2. *Arms*

The more turns you do, the stronger and more stable your arm position needs to be. So the dancers can begin to include the 'Campbell Technique', moving their arms through second to en avant to optimise pace and improve how aerodynamic the position is.

3. *Spotting*

There is of course the need for more head movements when we do more turns. Often the rhythm and psychology techniques for breaking the habit actually eradicate the need to focus purely on implementing further head rotations. However, it's always important to refocus on the spotting techniques when the focus shifts to doing more turns. Putting into practice the 'three heads for two turns' idea, as well as using visual targets, can never be overused when practising.

4. *Hopping*

Say, what? I'm asking you to let your dancer hop around that extra turn? Surely this goes against everything this book stands for! Controversially this does actually help. The habit is formed in the body knowing what a turn feels like; break that habit by making the body rotate one more time. Whether it is by hopping around, or joining the feet to soutenu, it doesn't matter; get the body around again and again.

For psychology there is a whole bunch of imagery and vocal stimuli we can use to mentally alter the habit.

Some are blatantly obvious...

'DON'T PUT YOUR FOOT DOWN.'
'KEEP YOUR FOOT STUCK TO YOUR LEG LONGER.'

Yelling these doesn't always work. In reality they probably don't make much difference to the dancer at all! It all boils down to being creative with your imagery again and using props. I love a prop! My mother, a studio owner, hates that I do, as after one of my classes there are Thera-Bands, blocks, teddy bears and literally anything I can find thrown around the room to tidy away!

Some examples of my tools to get that dancer breaking their habit…

1. Crocodiles

Probably most suited for the younger child that can imaginatively still believe this: 'If you put your foot down before you've done 'x' number of pirouettes you will lose a toe! How many toes will you go home with?' (Do not do this with the literal and nervous child!)

(Rosina's way – Get down on the floor and be the crocodile, snapping around their ankles!)

2. Paint up your leg

We've all used this spiel and maybe, if you dance on dirty floors, you may have the actual marks on your tights to prove it. Ask your dancers to lift their foot higher after 'x' amount of turns to do one more with their foot 2cm higher. This also helps re-engage the quadriceps, hamstring and glute muscles to secure the position, and helps them think of something opposite to their normal lowering of the leg.

(Rosina's way – Get some paint, firstly checking the children are not allergic, maybe even getting the parents to sign something. Oh, don't we love the twenty-first century! On bare legs try the theory out. Put a tiny little bit of paint on the outside of the big toe in parallel, or on the outside of the little toe for turned out, and get pirouette painting!

3. Take a video

Again, a well-used dance image, 'Imagine I am taking a photo', but who actually has? (OK, maybe more than there used to be judging by studio Instagram profiles!) Get the kids involved and let them use their phones to video, maybe even do it in slow motion! Becoming involved will see a change in the dancer's understanding.

If none of these ideas work to get your dancer to break their habits sometimes the warning of, 'Go around one more time or I'll spin you,' gets them turning quite well! Then the fear is broken and the habit can be worked on! Often then the teaching has to go right back to the start of training exercises! Young dancers are inconsistent... and that's why we love them... right?

Clapping

People often need a stimulus to connect the change of a habit to the movement. When giving up smoking, people decide that every time they would usually reach for a cigarette they swap that with a different item, a physical stimulus to maintain the change rather than just a mental thought. A sound often helps the dancers connect the correction with the movement. It takes a while to get the clap at the correct timing but often the stimulus makes a massive difference to the function of the correction, just by highlighting exactly where the correction should be applied.

Times where clapping is useful:

1. If a dancer often lets their supporting heel drop in the later turns, tell them to engage power down and push the floor away more at the point the heel usually gets lower, often after the third or fourth turn. You can use the Hard Ankle analogy too (Spaghetti Legs).

    When to clap: As a teacher clap at the point you have just highlighted to the dancer. This strategy can be used with any correction that gets worse throughout the turns, e.g. the lowering of the passé leg, the lowering of the arms, the bending of the underneath leg.
2. Moving the head. Often dancers know that they are meant to be spotting but coordinating the timing so that the head is the last thing to move often gets confusing, especially for the conscientious

dancer who is perhaps not a natural turner, focusing so hard on all the instructions but actually making the rotations harder by moving the head at an awkward time.

When to clap: Not when you want the dancer to be facing the front but when you want the dancer to move their head, often when the body is facing the back.

3. Training in America has a different sort of energy to the UK. The infectious energy in the classes and support for fellow dancers is second to none. I therefore always encourage clapping after a success or performance in a class. My students do it automatically and at workshops I always initiate clapping within the classes. Even if it's just to elevate the student who finally went the correct way in their turn, let alone worrying about the perfection of the position. So, in the immortal words of *Kinky Boots* the musical, 'Celebrate you to elevate you'. Introduce some clapping into your classes.

3. THE TURN AND ITS VARIATIONS

Turned Out!

The main focus of this book has been on parallel turns. I am a jazz and contemporary teacher, therefore these are the foremost turns I use and have witnessed going wrong. Pirouette Surgery® can be fully applied to the turned out ballerina too. The principles of core, centre of gravity, use of arms, spot and momentum are exactly the same; the difference is the preparation and the positioning of the legs. To drive these forward another level, these can also be taken on pointe. Often I work with young dancers who are at full-time ballet school. When only turned out is required it is important to only train the body in turnout, allowing the muscle memory control. This is where versatile young dancers have a harder job than those focusing purely on ballet. These dancers are required to turn both ways, so double the focus will be needed on the positioning and practice to allow neither style to be favoured or enhanced.

En Dedans – The Inside Turn

This involves turning towards the standing leg and is preferred to start in a long lunged (possibly a plunging lunged) fourth position. Many young dancers prefer this and in the younger classes this is often seen when you ask little people to 'spin'.

Alongside a lot of ballet training, which this book is not about, there are a couple of things I like dancers to practise when trying to perfect this turn. I often introduce this turn at a later stage and once those turns en dehors are consistent. In the initial action outwards, we stress the importance of the leg not pre-empting the body, but in an inward turn the body has to slightly pre-empt the leg, especially if you are doing an en dedans turn without the momentum of a fouetté of the leg. A dancer's COG is lower and further back in a lunged preparation, although it is important for the dancers to remember that most of the weight needs to be on the front foot. Due to this alteration of the COG the strength in the core and the glute muscle, as well as the perception of space, needs to be greater in order for the turn to hit perfect balance. The foot of an en dedans turn comes down in front and can technically lower to relevé fifth first, as opposed to an outward turn where a dancer is looking for suspension on the supporting leg and the leg is lowered gently down behind.

Gymnasts often turn inwards. I believe this to be because whilst turning inwards the weight continues forward from the preparation and stepping forwards on to a beam is easier than trying to find it backwards. You can always tell a gymnast in a dance class, during their leaps, their turns and their transitions they're beautifully pulled up and strong, but, more often than not, looking at the floor. I guess that's years of training on a four-inch wide beam, four feet off of the floor!

Pointe

In order to balance on pointe shoes a dancer's centre of gravity must be directly above the area of support. Unlike on demi-pointe where the dancer could just about manage the demi-pointe being around a centimetre off the floor in a weak rise, on a pointe shoe there is minimal space for an incomplete rise. We all know if you don't hit the block the movement will be redundant!

There is less torque in a pointe shoe: at the start, due to the turned out preparation; during, as the area of friction on the block is smaller and then also from the material of the shoe. Therefore, if a pirouette on pointe is perfect, its turn will be faster and smoother due to less friction, but the dancer will not necessarily do more turns, as the starting force will be less.

The reaction time for the relevé on pointe has to be much quicker; the toe must come right under the mass of the body. Training dancers to understand their COG and how it effects their turns will help them learn their optimum placement for balance.

Leg Grabs!

Evolved from rhythmic gymnastics, these are appearing in dance and on Instagram often enough for our young dancers to want to try them. A leg grab turn is very difficult.

In the view of physics, if your dancer is particularly flexible this position is optimum for momentum, as the inertia and radius is quite small.

This will only be the case however if your dancers are flexible enough to get their leg perpendicular to the floor, with a straight back, therefore creating a perfectly vertical axis. Any stiffness in the hamstring and misplacement of a tucked pelvis will affect this axis.

As well as extreme flexibility in this position, dancers also need to have a very strong core and back, and particularly tough arm muscles in order to maintain the pull whilst turning, as the once the leg falls lower down, there is more friction from the air and the pull is harder to maintain.

These can be taken both en dedans and en dehors. In both directions, focus on core and the ability to move the body as one, is vitally important. Locking down the top half of the body whilst engaging the arms to pull the leg, is also advantageous to the straight-line position. Dancers should work on the opposite arm reaching to the arch of the foot and the other grabbing mid calf in order to get enough leverage and the feeling of a 'lighter' leg.

Getting the leg up to its maximum position must be done quickly and the dancers must maintain length in the torso in order to turn smoothly.

Other than practising the leg grabs without the turn, firstly lying on the floor and then standing, these turns happen with utmost focus on suppleness and strength. Dancers are unable to spot well whilst their legs and arms are in the air, so the feeling of the shoulders and pelvis doing the rotating is very important.

On a Rake

Although there is only one show in the UK that requires a triple turn (*Fame*) many of the dance tracks in the musicals both touring and in the West End are performed in theatres with stages that are raked. (Usually found in older theatres where the stage slopes down towards the front.) This makes the pirouettes in the choreography harder, especially for the girls dancing in heels too. Counterbalance would be required to securely perform pirouettes on a rake. It is probably the only time where a bent in arm position would aid the success of the rotation. Dancers would need to train their body to turn with their COG in a slightly further back location.

À la Secondes!

There is a reason fouettés don't appear in grade 2 ballet! This move not only needs the ability to spin and balance, but for the dancer to also be able to maintain a technical and balletic turnout position with the legs. YouTube has enhanced the popularity of these turns. 'À la secondes', 'fouettés without a bend', 'boy fouettés', 'the *Billy Elliot* turns', 'pump turns' and all the other aliases these go by, are actually very difficult. They are not something that I focus on in Pirouette Surgery® workshops. This is because the success of these relies solely upon the principles of a basic pirouette; balance, positioning, core control and spotting; plus years of work and corrections from good ballet teachers in thousands of ballet classes!

À la secondes are very easy to practise wrong and then really hard to correct once momentum and ease has been felt and implanted in the wrong position.

I start preparation exercises for these with eight-year-olds* who are aware, although probably unable to consistently demonstrate, where their seconde position is. They do at least understand the process of turnout. We do a lot of exercises with a friend, their leg on a chair and at the barre before we attempt the turn. After originally learning these I revisit them regularly, but not too much to instil bad habits, especially if the placement of á la seconde isn't yet consistent! Like many things in adage, the higher the leg the easier it is to hold and this is apparent with these turns too. Not only does the leg appear to become lighter at and above the 90-degree position but it also then become a stabilising horizontal axis for the turns.

Please note these are not beginner eight-year-olds. These are ones that have danced since they were five and attended ballet for around three years.

Legs aside (no pun intended), there is much more to the successes of an á la seconde turn than the leg position. The preparation, the directional focus and arm coordination plays a big role in the triumph of all kinds of pirouettes, but especially in these.

The preparation for these turns is highly important. These turns are quite strange. Ultimately our á la seconde turns are performed with both legs in turnout, however when we observe the videos of children in the United States demonstrating these turns (I'm pretty sure that is where this trend began!), the preparation is from parallel. I find that from a parallel jazz fourth position there is further torque into the turn, as often turnout dancers cheat and don't keep the whole foot on the floor (therefore the turning force is coming from the inside of the big toe as opposed to the whole ball of the foot). How this is taught is down to aesthetics and teachers' personal choice. It is extremely difficult to hold anything in turnout, so that is the correction most young dancers get. The supporting leg is often completely parallel too, so it is vital that dancers strengthen their inner thighs and be aware of how the two legs relate to each other in a movement. I like to use a syncopated rhythm, '8 &', to start off these turns, it gets the ball rolling. The first movement is massively important to the success of these turns, so I train this part over and over again.

Once prepared in either parallel or turned out fourth, the first movement, called the 'switch' by Krista Miller, joins the arms together in en avant from their preparation position. At the same time as this arm movement, the body makes a three quarter turn with the leg in a low position, rotating the leg to croisé. At this point the dancers are then in croisé with the working leg in en avant and the supporting leg in fondu. Arms are first position too.

Common practice in fouetté teaching is to finish the rotation to the corner; momentum then carries the dancer around to face completely to the front. It is important for dancers to understand that their focus never spots the corner, but moves into centre front. Training their bodies to aim for the corner each time allows the dancers to successfully look like they're turning square on each time because they don't overshoot the front with the momentum that is gathered whilst turning.

The dancers have now done the first part of the turn on the count '&'. In the next part the dancers pull up to full relevé with the supporting leg braced, whilst the other leg moves to second. The arms move to second at the same time and the dancer completes one whole turn, returning back on to fondu facing croisé.

Depending on the level of dancers, I often make them demonstrate one turn '& 1' and then hold the croisé on the next '&' without continuing momentum on further turns, as this focuses them purely on their core strength and how that formulates the turn, as opposed to bodily momentum. Similar to practising basic pirouette position, the process of just one turn, with the correct action of the underneath leg, arms, use of core and head spot, cannot be practised enough. Even with the most advanced dancers, going back to basics can be of great assistance.

If you want your dancers to turn like an army, teach them like an army, all of them must be able to do the preparation properly without moving on to the next rotations. This is something I noticed happens in many American and Australian jazz classes. Until all the children can kick at 90 degrees none of the more flexible children are allowed to kick any higher. Until the whole class can do a double turn, none of the natural turners can demonstrate three! How boring for the elite child I hear you say, but then this was in jazz preparation classes with six-year-olds!

In á la seconde turns many of the pointers of basic pirouettes apply. Specifically the Spaghetti Legs sections, as well as the Michael Jackson pelvis movement, play a massive role in the development and improvement of these turns. The use of a strong core and biomechanical connection also helps these turns develop.

In order to teach balletic fouettés with the whipping bend-around-straight movement of the leg, all principles of basic turning technique must be applied with even more focus on the ballet values, especially involving the turnout. On first observance the moving leg looks as if it circles, when it is more of a rond de jambe en l'air movement. Never do the dancers want their thigh to move behind their body line. Telling dancers to draw a D often removes the cancan action! This isn't #FouettéSurgery though and I think I could write another whole book on those!

We will all agree, when done well, both á la secondes and fouettés are great, but when done badly, they're horrid! Although, as always with children, my mantra is 'one day they'll get there', in the meantime we as teachers must let go of some of the detail, open our minds and possibly close our eyes, as iconic moves are murdered by our ten-year-old ballet recreational dancers! Rome wasn't built in a day and perfect technique wasn't cultivated in an hour!

Coordinating the arms and the legs without too much force is optimum for these kinds of turns. Too much force and arms and legs working against each other will definitely end in the dancer falling over!

There are two exercises I do to instil the arm coordination of these turns. Aiming for the arms in á la seconde when they're on their demi-pointe and when in croisé and the underneath leg is on fondu then the arms in en avant.

1. *Clap and splat*

From the preparation get the children to clap when they fondu and then open their arms to second. You can do this with them when they're not turning.

2. *Slap the mat*

Closing the arms is quite an easy movement, opening them, which causes some air thrust isn't always favourable. Therefore I get two children to stand either side of the turner with two of those little pre-school marker mats, making sure they are slightly in front of their arms when they have full wingspan. The child turns and every time they hit the front coming up from fondu they have to slap the mat. Proprioception of the mats to the side soon develops, but don't worry too much about the technique of the slapping, or else you'll be trying to eradicate strange wrist movements!

Slap the mat!

3. *Pass the parcel*

For this I use quoits, they're easy to hold and lightweight. Aimed at the advanced dancer who is quite competent with their turns, but struggles with their arm coordination. With the quoit, or any other object, start with the object in the front arm and then on every fondu swap the quoit to the opposite hand. This really makes the dancer think of their arms and helps the turns become more consistent. It's also quite fun and sometimes the object flies off around the room, so perhaps a baby brother isn't the best item to use in this exercise!

Travelling Turns

Often the best place to start with little ones is with travelling turns. These involve much more natural movement processes than preparing and standing on one leg! The children also seem to have much more fun travelling them, without really knowing what they are working on.

Whatever age my students are we start the classes with the famous Royal Ballet Junior Associate audition exercise of skipping in a circle down from each corner.

This exercise really helps the dancers use their whole body to create the rotation, hands are best kept on the hips to keep the shoulders down and allow the head sufficient space to move and spot.

You can also do this with galloping and springing.

Gallops

They can do one by half turning then the next completing the turn. Springing is an easier option than the skips, especially with younger children. We all know the hardest things to teach are 'skips'!

Posé Turns

Whilst these enter ballet syllabi at an advanced level, the inward spin action is a more natural movement than the outward one. When we first start teaching pirouettes many children turn in front of us inward, rather than outward, so another good place to start with turning is this exercise. Remember to use the obvious ballet technical build-ups and teaching methods to teach these. My juniors absolutely love a posé turn!

Chaînés

They are the most effective-looking turn. They're the turn that your Uncle Jim tries to demonstrate after too many whiskies at a Wedding. But, they are excellent exercise for all ages. In order to turn in a straight line the dancers' cores must be completely engaged. A slight lean back and the chaînés will go around in a circle, and a slight lean forward and it will travel the other way. Chaînés are an excellent way for dancers to find their personal centre of gravity. Starting slow is always best! I will always remember the first time I had a go at chaînés; I was at my associate programme class, around 11 years old, and we attempted to stay in between some wooden floorboards all the way along the room. I cannot remember a lot of focus on the positioning of the legs, but I can remember the teacher demonstrating and then us giving it a good go! It was a Christmas special class, if I remember rightly, but what I've learnt from this is that we should just let kids try things. It was interesting to hear that Autumn Miller teaches her tots how to chaîné. It seems a far off concept to get our four-year-olds turning and travelling, however once a dancer's chaînés are strong, everything is strong. The action of turning the whole body as one piece, staying high up on their demi-pointe and using their arms as stabilisation is drastically important. I always say to myself, never underestimate kids, and whilst it's highly unlikely your preschoolers will turn en menage by six years old, their proprioception and awareness of their body will definitely improve.

Applying all Pirouette Surgery® drills for spotting, relaxed necks, arm placement, muscular connection and momentum apply to all sorts of turns: inwards, outwards, travelling or static, balletic or jazz.

4. PIROUETTE SURGERY® AILMENT CHART

At the end of every Pirouette Surgery® class the dancers have the opportunity to show me their turns one by one and I give them a correction or two, or a hundred!

It takes practice to be able to select the main detrimental factor to dancers' turns and they are often unique. Whilst it would be lovely to be able to diagnose the turns of every dancer that manages to read this book, I have created the chart below (which is also available in the dance teachers' manual) of the most common ailments of a dancer's turns and which parts of this book to refer to when trying to correct them.

As a form of reference to teachers and dancers, I hope this section helps you find specific corrections to help your turns improve.

Alternatively, if this doesn't help you send me a video or... book a Pirouette Surgery® masterclass!

What is going wrong?	Reason	Chapter/idea to reference
Dancers are putting their heels down.	• Habit. • Leg strength is weak.	Kicking the Habit. Spaghetti Legs. Hard Ankle.
Dancers are not moving their heads.	• Neck tension. • Hairstyles.	Spotting.
Dancers look like they are moving in separate parts. Hips, then torso, then head.	• Lack of position strength. • Pre-empting of turn on front foot and opening hips.	Sellotape Phenomenon, using the Seat Belt Torso idea to turn. Goldilocks Complex, initial dynamic phase.

What is going wrong?	Reason	Chapter/idea to reference
Dancers are leaning backward.	• Arms are too bent. • Are lacking core stability.	*T. Rex* Can't Turn. Core training exercises
Dancers are falling forward.	• Arms are too low or long. • Spotting the floor. • Habitual movement.	*T. Rex* Can't Turn. Head alignment. Kicking the Habit.
Dancers are moving their head through tilted angles.	• Loose hair. • Focusing too much on the whip.	Spotting imagery – Head floating on water.
Dancers are falling sideways.	• Preparation is too big. • Hip is lifted.	Goldilocks Complex. Spaghetti Legs – the supporting leg.
Dancers are turning the wrong way.	• Don't know how to turn, revert to natural movement.	Wheeeeeeeeee Factor – Thumb Slap preparation.
Dancers are not spinning fast enough.	• Fear. • Lacking torso connection. • Preparation is disconnected.	Wheeeeeeeeee Factor. Sellotape Phenomenon.

What is going wrong?	Reason	Chapter/idea to reference
Dancers are on a low relevé.	• Weak ankles or glute muscles. • Dancers have gained muscle memory on a TurnBoard.	Spaghetti Legs.
Dancers' arms are lifting up and shoulders rounding.	• Latissimus dorsi and back muscles are not connected.	Find Your Wings.
Dancers are rounding their lumbar spine in order to engage their abdominals.	• Unclear about core properties.	Lego Bricks.
Dancers appear to be spinning uncontrollably.	• Dancers are using momentum instead of strength.	Rhythm and Breathing.
Dancers struggle to complete the whole turn.	• Lacking perception of where the front is or what a whole turn feels like.	So Close, Yet So Far.
Dancers struggle to get much force at the start of turn.	• Preparation is too wide or turned out. • Slipping.	Goldilocks Complex. Bare foot.
Dancer's lifted knee drops and foot goes behind the knee.	• Lack of practice in the position.	Sellotape Phenomenon with the invisible muscle. Core exercises.
Dancers look rigid.	• No breathing. • Posture isn't dynamic.	Sellotape Phenomenon.

What is going wrong?	Reason	Chapter/idea to reference
Dancers lose the correct positioning.	• Muscle memory is not strong enough to maintain during rotations.	Sellotape Phenomenon. Teaching Manual.
Dancer's arms position is too long.	• Dancers relate the movement to ballet.	*T. Rex* Can't Turn.
Dancer's arms are bent in.	• Habitual movement.	*T. Rex* Can't Turn.
Dancer's jazz fourth is too deep.	• Not using dynamic power but instead fatigued.	Goldilocks Complex.
Dancers twist their bodies to get more turns. Preparation arms go behind the spine.	• Not using the core to turn but the arms.	Seat Belt exercise.
Dancers change their spots.	• Not focused on one point and often distracted. • Dependent upon eyesight also.	Teacher placement and Spotting.
Dancers rest the toe on the leg.	• Using the structure of the body to hold the position as opposed to the muscular connection.	Spaghetti Legs – The working leg.
Dancer's leg creeps up to the position.	• Slow reaction to the position. Whilst this doesn't affect the consistency of turns it loses torque at the start so less turns.	Initial reaction phase.

What is going wrong?	Reason	Chapter/idea to reference
Dancers' heads are protruding forward.	• Trying too hard to spot.	Epic Stare.
Dancers jump up to the relevé position.	• Lacking downward connection into the floor.	Spaghetti Legs.
Dancers say that they can't do it.	• Dependent on teachers' approach to turns and also the students' past experiences.	It's All in the Mind.
Dancer's turns finish suddenly.	• Working on momentum instead of strength.	Spaghetti Legs and working on maintaining the stop and hover.
Dancer's preparation is in turned out and the turn parallel, or vice versa.	• Poor proprioception. Habitual action. • Weak glutes to maintain leg alignment.	Preparation drills. Teacher focus.
Dancers run out of momentum.	• Creating further torque in the body and legs.	Leg strengthening and core exercises.
Dancers turn on low relevé.	• Counterbalancing a displacement of pelvis and core posture.	Positioning and core exercises.

Turning During Growth Spurts

We all know how much the adolescent growth spurt can affect our dancers! One day it all appears to be coming together and then the next they're like a giraffe on ice. That once tight positioned double pirouetter is falling off balance.

Luckily, unlike some other sports, or in fact other elements of dance, the pirouette isn't too dangerous for children's bones. During growth spurts, children's bones are at their weakest and it is also a time when bones are growing a lot faster than muscles. This results in tight ligaments and loss of muscle strength, often leading to injuries. Whilst we must remember this when stretching our dancers during this time we can be quite safe to continue practising pirouettes.

However, because of their rapid growth the dancer's awareness of where their body will be becomes more difficult, as well as the coordination and sustainable use of power in the legs. With the lack of balance injuries are susceptible and for that reason we must be careful with our dancers at this age. It is therefore massively important to continue focusing on strength training, especially movement-based strength exercises (such as squatting, lunging, jumping) and also remember the important role confidence plays in turns.

Between the ages of 11-14 is an awesome time to go back to basics with turning exercises, rebuilding the technique during the growth spurt and also reinstilling confidence.

There is science behind how this affects pirouettes too, Hayri Baran Yosmaoğlu from Baskent University, Faculty of Health Science, Department of Physiotherapy and Rehabilitation, Turkey, states within his book *Proprioception: The forgotten Sixth Sense* that:

As a result of this rapid change [adolescent growth spurt], *since the necessary force amount would increase especially in rotational movements, it is quite possible to have adaptation problem in sensory-motor system during planning the movement. This situation may cause decrease in success especially in movements which require high coordination. Furthermore, orientation and segmental stabilization were analyzed at the head, shoulder, trunk, and pelvis level and it is reported proprioceptive neglect in sensory integration of postural control in adolescence period.*[17]

In other words, this explains that a growth spurt affects dancer's preparations and then the reaction time it takes to coordinate a movement. Highlighting that the connection between the head, shoulders, trunk and pelvis is weaker and there is less stability with posture. Reaction time and posture are massive parts to a successful pirouette.

R. K. Jensen also pointed out; 'That during growth spurt, moment of inertia increased 46% in transverse axis.'[18]

Forty-six per cent, whoa! It just goes to show how small a change in inertia can change the pirouette! Imagine being 46% wider... it doesn't bear thinking about!

However, this again highlights that the most optimum amount of turns with a small moment of inertia, therefore a nice fast turn, will not be achievable during growth spurt time.

My best advice is to get your dancers turning pre-growth spurt, then use that unstable time to reinstall technique to hopefully come out the other side still a great turner. Again this highlights a problem to me with the average age to start turns in this country, which was 11. Why are we starting dancers training on one of the most difficult moves when at the same time they're managing massive changes physically too?

17   Yosmaoğlu, H. (2015). *Proprioception: The forgotten sixth sense.* Foster City, USA: Omits Groups Ebooks, p.2.

18   Jensen, R. K. (1981) The effect of a 12-month growth period on the body moments of inertia of children. Med. Sci. Sports Exerc. 13: 238-242.

5. ADDING TURNING TO YOUR CLASSES

Turns should be introduced as something fun, but unfortunately they haven't been in the past. We currently have *Generation Dance Moms* (for those of you that have not been exposed to *Dance Moms*, it is a reality TV show following a studio, its teacher and a group of elite dancers in America), the pre-professional dance world's current 11-13-year-olds. These are kids that were brought up with YouTube and social media at their fingertips. No longer do they need to go to the Royal Opera House to see a dancer perform 32 fouettés, this can be found within seconds on the Internet. The inspiration is right there. So this generation of children are the ones that began tiptoeing their way into the world of turns, tricks and leaps by practising alone and basic instinctual learning (aka copying) at home. Teachers also observed the expertise and skill of younger dancers on the Internet and television, and began to push their dancers beyond what they used to expect from them. Some teachers are adamant that they will remain old school and haven't given in to Americanising the way they teach the children, however there is a fine line between pushing boundaries within teaching and going too far. The schools with the over split torture devices, those that teach a back handspring before petit jetés, I feel have gone too far. However in a consumer led industry, we must offer what the client wants! If we don't offer it, in a safe and instructed environment, then our young dancers will just go home and find a YouTube tutorial to teach them instead.

I spoke to some of the important people from dance examination boards in the UK, asking them why turning preparation exercises are so absent from their syllabuses and then when turns are finally introduced are touched upon so briefly. Their answer was that turning preparation was up to their teachers to supplement in free work etc. So, if it is down to the teachers themselves then it will happen in some places but not others which therefore highlights the range of dance standards that we see across the country.

On the road to success, confidence is paramount. It takes time to build confidence and also to be able to use it proficiently for the outcome we want in any situation, rather than where we are most comfortable. Back to the Italian learning, in class and in a comfortable environment my speaking is comprehensible, yet in a situation where I am not comfortable I can only process basic sentences. The same is apparent for turns and the reason Pirouette Surgery® began was to make turns comfortable and therefore more successful. In order for dancers to become comfortable with turns, exposing youngsters to turning techniques is paramount. But when is too young? In America, they turn in tots' classes, but the amount of training is very different there to here in the UK. Our six to seven-year-old dancers perhaps train twice a week for an hour; in the US serious dancers are already training nearly every night of the week. There is less focus on passing examinations and learning syllabi routines and instead focus on drills and training exercises. The UK has a very set method for improvement and exams are still vitally important to many students and parents as a means of acknowledging development. I like to start dancers off with the basics of turning and Level 1 exercises when they are five and six years old. By nine, pre-secondary school, I expect them to be able to perform triple turns, and beyond that age to continue the development of more rotations and further understanding of forces and motion for consistency. By 13, their knowledge of how to turn should be complete, as I have found that post this age the number of additional rotations begins to show less of an increase.

It is noted by Andrew Hamilton of Peak Performance that:

Between the ages of 8-12 a child is ripe for learning of skills (and knowledge). Teach the right skills at this time and the child will become a physically gifted adult, but teach them wrongly and it will be at best a difficult struggle to unravel them in future to produce optimum performance.

With the accessibility of YouTube and dancers wanting to be just like those on *Dance Moms*, studios have seen the demand and subsequent expansion of classes in their studios to include those such as acrobatics.

To see an improvement of turns, specialist-turning classes should be included in studios' timetables too. American studios offer leaps and turns classes, not only at the larger drop-in establishments (Broadway Dance Center, EDGE Performing Arts Center etc.) but the local dance studios too.

Understandably adding in another class to a studio's timetable is never the easiest of tasks, however with the introduction of a turning class many age groups can go together so at first. Whilst all the basics are practised, dancers can learn their turns and the drills all together. Once standards improve and newer students begin, classes would then need to be split. Whilst I do not own a studio myself, I do artistically direct one, and the supplementary drop-in classes to the normal syllabus and free work classes have been a massive hit. Not only does the studio's income benefit, but also the students improve. These drop-in classes are paid for separately and accessed through a class card system, attendance isn't mandatory, and dancers can attend whichever drop-in classes they wish. A turns class could be added to your studio like this. Alternatively placing a 30-minute turns class in between two modern classes and offering a deal that the turns class is only £x extra if you attend the modern class, would also be a lucrative way to add turning to your schedule.

(I'm hoping my next endeavour is #StudioSurgery™... I'm very excited to share how having a dance studio is a passion and a hobby but must always be a business too.)

Turns take practise, and practise takes time, so I personally do not think that applying the ideas written about in this book within your regular classes, and not focusing on turns separately, will allow you to see as big an improvement as is possible in your students' turning skills. So depending on how much of an improvement you want to see, I offer you two options. I am qualified, but not affiliated to any specific exam board, the classes that I teach are not based on any syllabus and I have no problem teaching workshops at studios from all different exam boards and strategies. (Even though I have the ISTD in my blood and my newly married initials spell RAD... Ironic?) Therefore my book is not affiliated or endorsed by any teaching association and never will be. I want its ideas and drills to be available to all, whatever the style, whatever the exam board and whatever the country. As I have worked in studios in many countries I cannot begin to explain the importance of sharing ideas with other dancers and other worldly cultures.

Option 1 – Read this book, take its ideas and add them to your own turning classes. There are some example exercises throughout the book.

Option 2 – In addition to this book I have written my Three Level Programme of Pirouette Drills and Exercises. For a one-off fee, you will be licensed to duplicate the syllabus drills and exercises within your studio and add Pirouette Surgery® to your timetable. Once registered, additional articles and developmental exercises for more advanced turns will follow throughout the year. There are also online videos with all exercises demonstrated.

Teachers: If you have bought this book and didn't order the teachers' manual, but now would like to buy it, please drop me and email stating the dance studio at which you teach and Pirouette29 to be given the link to purchase the teachers' manual separately without repurchasing this book.

(*Option 3* – Book me for a workshop! Brazen self-promotion, sorry!)

How you choose to use this book and my ideas is completely down to you. I just want turns to be accessible to all and the UK to turn. Whether the successes of the country's young dancers' spinning depends on your own version of my ideas, or you trust me and use my ideas, that's for you to decide.

I always say, 'the best compliment someone can give you, is copying you!'

What's next for Rosina?

Rosina is holding the first of her teachers intensives this coming summer before her annual Elite Collaborative Summer School. She hopes to continue the 'Surgery' series with a line of E-book add on chapters; Studio Surgery™, Leap Surgery™, Stretch Surgery™, Parent Surgery™, Imagery Surgery™.

She will be presenting her methods at some of the worlds largest dance conventions and continuing her touring workshops with Sam. There is another big dream of theirs...but by putting that in print it definitely would be copied...you'll just have to wait and see!

All information can be found on Rosina's website www.rosinaandrews. co.uk and her social media; Facebook: Rosina Andrews Dancer Choreographer Teacher and Twitter/Instagram: @rosiniballerini

6. LET'S TALK TURNS

Exclusive Interviews

All statements were correct at the time of print, April 2016.

With Krista Miller and Autumn Miller

Autumn and Krista Miller

I have watched Autumn for many years on YouTube and have seen her flawless technique, so managing to coordinate a meeting with her and her master trainer mum was a dream come true. Both of them have a wealth of knowledge and Krista truly is a dance master trainer.

Name – Krista Miller (K) and Autumn Miller (A)
Current title/Company –
K - KBM Talent, Master Trainer.
A - National champion and Internet sensation

Background:

Krista Miller is the owner of KBM Talent and mother of two. She began her professional career as a Los Angeles Laker Girl and has since gone on to work in commercials, television and film. Some of her credits include dancing with Jim Carrey in the movie *The Mask*, *North*, a Rob Reiner film, *Happy Hour*, *Saved by the Bell*, *Jackass Number Two* and the TV-made movie *Cinderella*.

She has performed with numerous artists such as Prince, The Bare

Naked Ladies, Fastball, Elvis Costello, CeCe Winans and the Pussycat Dolls. Her most recent choreography can be seen in the recent film *The Dukes* and the live Skechers show.

With her passion for dance, her technical background and years of experience, she is described as one of the most sought-after dance teachers in the USA. She's likely to be seen now on her very popular teaching channel www.kbmtalent.com

Autumn Miller began dancing at the age of five and hasn't stopped since. She trains about 30 hours per week at Mather Dance Company in all styles of dance including jazz, contemporary, acro, hip-hop and ballet. Autumn also travels with KBM TALENT and assists her mom, Krista Miller, in Technique & Improve classes. Autumn is known for her very popular YouTube channel *AutiesFreestyleFriday* where she does fun dance videos, skits, teaches and lets her audience in on her personal dance journey. Autumn's *FreestyleFriday* currently has over 60 million views to date as well as over 700,000 followers on her personal Instagram account. Some of Autumn's credits include *Dancing with the Stars*, Disney's *Shake it Up*, Willow Smith's *Whip my Hair* music video, AwesomenessTV and the Fox hit show *Mobbed*.

How do you first go about teaching pirouettes to young jazz students?

Krista – For me, I think the hardest part with that is getting them to understand the body position, so when I start with them, I would start with basic holding in the passé position. Making sure that the passé position is correct and it is high and the foot isn't sickled and different things like that. Basically, just getting them to understand going into that from fourth position and holding that balance. Staying on flat foot for a bit and maybe trying to relevé. This is how we would start in any of the basic jazz classes. Getting them to understand rotations or going back even further, of course you're going to go right into your chaîné turns in those baby classes to get them to understand spotting and rotating, but I wouldn't start with the pirouetting that young because the balance is so confusing which then affects the body position.

You say chaîné turns; do children do those really young?

K – Very young, the very first thing we teach them.

Autumn – I teach the little babies at our studio and they're three and four, and they have chaîné like *click, click*. That's the first thing I taught them.

K – Honestly, it's usually pretty bad at the beginning. The spotting is pretty confusing too, we have pictures and it says things like 'Stop'. So they have to say the word when they see it. They don't know how to do a pirouette but they know the feeling of rotation and of spot, so when it gets to it and their motor skills are ready, they should be able to turn, if you build it right in.

How old would you begin training for pirouettes specifically?

A – When we do pirouettes we basically start at about six, probably.

K – I would say the 'five's are doing them,

A – But when you're actually getting more than one turn, they're about six.

As dancers get older how does your focus on the technical elements change?

K – For me body position is number one, so what I try to do by when they're eight or nine, I explain the importance of breathing, and how to build the core muscles and the strength of the stomach. As before that, when they're three or four, we still do sit-ups but it's just a bunch of head nodding. So we think about balance as they get older. They can't comprehend it too young but to think about it I explain it like an apple. The kids all have those fancy apple cutters that the mom or dad pushes down and then all the pieces of the apple open up and I say 'what is left?' The core is left and so if those pieces are gone the only thing left standing is the core. The only thing in order to finish those turns at the end really is the core muscles. Autumn is now beginning to relate what her core does to her dance movements. Breathing during the sit-up process is key for me, in through the nose, out through the mouth, the correct way, which I am sure that Sam, your husband, knows about!

I remember my ballet teacher would say to me 'Close your ribs, suck in, tuck under' and I used to think I don't even know what that means. I would just stand there for so long that, eventually, as I realised breath came out of the mouth, the ribcage would close. So, as you're able to keep the ribcage locked and closed like that, the back will stay straight and the only way to reinforce those muscles is through breathing to strengthen. You want your six-pack right and then you've got to strengthen the obliques and then the muscles that wrap around the sides as well holding the back. My biggest thing is when the kids get into harder turns, coupés or anything, they start to release their stomach muscles and they fall out of it. So if you can actually figure out a way, and the only way I've been able to get them to hold it, is through sit-ups, cross core and planks. We do a lot of that. I base my entire warm-up on core and balance. Stretching is fabulous, but once they figure out the core, they can pretty much do anything. Once you can balance and hold forever and ever and ever, the body is in the right spot and the dancer is in control. This is my number one focus when they are older. Then of course I'd build into all the other things, arm placement, spot, but core is for sure the number one thing. Once that's in the right place everything is in the right place. The Pilates and the conditioning are huge; Autumn does a whole hour strength and conditioning class once a week and then we have cardio classes too.

The doctor said to Autumn with her current injury [strained back], if her body wasn't in the shape it is and the way she's been taking care of it, this injury would take four – six weeks, but we are going to be able to narrow the time down to two – three weeks and then she'll be back on her way because of the way she has trained. Injuries are serious so it's important to try to strengthen to eradicate the risks.

The back is so popular here at the moment; the dance world is so different. When I was training the technical portion with the turns etc. was so important and now it's definitely acro and rhythmic.

Rosina – The UK loves to copy what they see on Instagram without any substance or understanding behind it. Sam and I really try not to do that.

Sam – When we do workshops together, these teachers say to me 'these kids can do 1,000 sit-ups' and I always say but can they do them properly? So I take them back to basics.

K – I say that about sit-ups too, let's do 100 good crunches and get the job done! Education is power and knowledge; you have to know about it! It's hard with social media today because everyone gets excited, 'I want to try that' and get my leg over my head, and I'm always like, 'Be careful!' It is so easy for students and teachers to get access to this, but it's also important to know how to teach it.

R – That 14 seconds doesn't show the six years of ballet training.

K – Right, the ballet, Ballet at least three times a week is important.

As a lot of teachers have different views on spotting and head whip, what are your views on spotting? How important is it and how do you teach it?

K – I'm not a massive whipper. But the one thing I will teach is natural rotation. As long as they can see themselves, or they physically see something on their face in the mirror, seeing is important, as they come around they usually can't focus. With little ones we hold up fingers, because what happens is they say they can see, but what they're actually seeing is a blur. I notice that the whipping of the head can get confusing and then their head dips and turns. Sometimes they drop their chin because that's how they think they can focus, so I like to say that they have an apple under their chin.

The spots need to be rotations not whips, that's how they use their head to get more turns. Sometimes they get so excited and stop, when often their body is still going, so that's why they need to allow the head to move in connection to their body, not separately. The faster they spot; it then takes the lead, without having to wind up the body. I don't believe in winding up in preparation. The legs give you the power, get the arms in and then the head whips hard, but not crazy fast. For me, the spotting is one of my least important issues with kids. As long as their neck is even and those eyes are in the mirror, that's enough spot for me.

Do you teach turns with a specific rhythm?

K – Nope! Not at all, once they're in the zone that's that. I count it evenly 1, 2, 3.

What do you think is the optimum preparation position for a pirouette?
(Everyone gets up and demonstrates around the table.)

K – When I was growing up, wide was cool! Back at Tremaine and all that! We now go straight back from parallel, as wide as your shoulders and pushing straight back, with a high demi-pointe at the back. If your heel is down with the weight back, you don't get enough power. Wide means you have to push off to come back to centre;

straight back and small, means you go straight up. Seems like the UK style hasn't evolved much from the eighties!

Arms?

K – I like arms lower.

A – The beach ball!

K – I think from the belly button out, lower, if you think of your belly button being halfway to the top and halfway to the bottom of your own body. So the centre is that; the core muscles are coming from there. The arms always want to come up. I find there is more power lower, but this everyone differs on. The arms definitely need to be rounded though, not flat.

Whilst turns don't make a good dancer, solid technique will always give a dancer freedom to do what they want to do! How much do you focus on technical purity alongside performance when you are training?

K –Probably 75% technique, then the performance has to be learnt to be done themselves. You can't really teach that. It comes from within. If you're technically your best and feeling strong, you'll always naturally feel better and able to perform. When they get older and into the 'contemporary storytelling world', a lot of the kids haven't experienced these things, so I find that is where it is hard – the technique stays, but the storytelling is harder. I try to get them to simulate what the audience should be feeling. I associate it with the game of charades. If the song is talking about the word love, what does that feel like it and how would they portray it?

Is acrobatics important to you?

K – I do not teach it. I can do it; I grew up doing basic gymnastics. I think it's great, it's a plus, but it's dangerous, you need the right kind of teacher to teach it! On the East Coast it's very big, everyone's doing chin stands and neck rolls, now it's more common here. We devote about one – two hours a week to it.

A – More gymnastics than acro. The acro is all the moves bending in half, although that's what dance seems to be now, you can do a straight scorpion in dance too. Gymnastics is more the tumbling so we split half and half.

K – The back stuff freaks me out. Kids' backs are different. Someone who is really flexi in their backs might not be in their legs. Just because you're flexi doesn't mean their back is flexible, you have to work different areas.

A – Some people are just born with their backs bent!

K – Autumn's had to work for back flexibility, for sure. She has good back but not overly bendy.

What inspires you?

K – What is exciting for me is that a lot of people don't teach technique so being able to go in and travel and teach different kids and actually see that little light bulb go 'ping'; it's exciting! Especially when you see progress. Dance is a work in progress and a journey, yet everyone wants those 16 turns tomorrow! Seeing progress inspires me to just keep going, including the notes and sweet emails from the teachers saying how much they've learnt. In a world that's selfie obsessed and me, me, me, it's really cool to be seen to be thanked. I also love to see Autumn go from beginning to end; at the start of the year and then seeing the progress at nationals in June or July. I see the kids every year get better and better. Travelling the world and seeing how different people do things is also really cool!

Did you train Autumn?

K – Yes, alongside a lot of the other teachers at the studio. The technical elements and the turns definitely; I can take the credit for those!

What is your advice for teachers?

K – Follow your gut, follow what you think is right, don't do the whole hype thing. Create a positive environment for the students, not everyone can do everything, and that's OK, but everyone can do it if you continue to encourage and nurture. Everyone is working towards different things; don't discard them because they're not there yet! I didn't grow up as a tapper, so I don't class myself as a tapper, but I kind of wish someone had pushed me and said you can do this.

Over to some questions for Autumn now! How old were you when you started dancing?

A – Well I was three, but I didn't really start training or competing until I was about six.

K – We were lucky if we got the shoes on before that time!

Do you remember when you first did turns?

A – I think they came naturally to me, because I'd seen a lot of people do them. I have a good visual memory because once I've seen something I'm able to try it. I have had some awesome teachers too, who have been able to show me every step. Turning for me was hard at first, I didn't even know what I was doing, everyone said I was spinning and I was like, 'What's spinning!' I guess I was six or seven, doing doubles etc. At seven definitely doing á la secondes.

K – And those at seven are not really normal! Eight is more the average age for those. If you're going do it, you should be doing those by then!

How long are your classes?

A – They're around one hour and a half, or two hours, especially for leaps and turns.

K – Any less than an hour you can't get anything done! Each year we like the kids' amount of turns to go up a number and the longer you can train them the better the muscle memory becomes.

Do you make modifications when you do more turns?

A – No not really. Maybe adding more plié. I do not change my arms like some people, although it does help to close them.

K – I'm not a fan of that as when they close their arms, their upper bodies collapse too. I try to stay open and wide. Controlling a nice double is much harder than doing more. Especially when you know you have the power.

What is your personal best turning amount?

A – Probably eight or nine, they're consistent daily. Once in a while ten. It's not a big deal to get ten turns, there's loads of people that can do it. The jump from five to seven or eight is more of a big deal.

K – You never get to do that many turns! In groups, four is probably the nice solid amount. And it has to be on relevé! You'll get more credit doing a good double on a high relevé, than doing a sloppy multiple. As a judge I wouldn't say anything about a perfect double, but doing more opens a lot of corrections up!

What is your favourite dance style?

A – I really like contemporary, you can do a lot of different things. Jazz is a lot of fun too! Ballet is good, everyone needs ballet; I take it!

Do you prefer jazz or ballet turns?

A – Definitely jazz, sometimes ballet ones in contemporary are pretty though.

**How do you stay up on relevé at the end of your turns,
it's so impressive?**

A – This I do not know, it's a difficult one! Closing the ribs to be solid is one of the biggest things. Even I like to open my ribs; it's one of my biggest corrections. Also, pushing up to the highest relevé straight away and staying there; holding that position strong, everything together.

How many hours do you train a week?

A – Probably 25 - 30. I'm homeschooled, so I get to go to the studio by two o'clock but I'm there every night until 10 or 10.30 p.m. The last two weeks before competitions, I was there 63 hours! It was a lot!

What are your long-term career goals?

A – That's a hard one, I really don't know. Having this journey already has been a dream come true! I've never thought, since I was six, that I would be where I am today. I think teaching dance, maybe getting a movie or something really cool. I love modelling and doing lots of fun things, so as long as I'm happy and I really don't have anything that I've set. It will come when it's meant to.

K – We've had an incredible run with the YouTube channels and worked with a lot of different companies. It's been wonderful. She's had a few things, with *Dancing with the Stars*, and Disney's, *Shake it Up*. Those opportunities will come around. Fourteen is a tricky age, not really a kid, not really an adult, so I think she's currently settled in training. I didn't have anything like this. My mum didn't know anything about the business and I didn't have an agent as a kid. I never really got to do it until my adult life and being able to transition into it was great. Having a technical background then was different though, as everything was transitioning into music videos, so back in the day when I was getting in, there wasn't the job base for technical dancers. There weren't contemporary companies or conventions; there was one Joe Tremaine. Nothing like it is now!

Convention life and social media have changed everything. I was lucky to get work then and work ever since. I know how much and how long you can do it for, so I don't want to push it on Autumn, she needs to have that long life. We get to travel and meet new people and those life experiences have been incredible. She's going to be a really good teacher too; she's so great with kids! Whatever God presents for us is the next journey, put your good energy out there and hope for the best.

Who started the YouTube channel?

K – It's a funny story… Back when Autumn was about eight, there was a little group called The Single Ladies. Autumn was one of the little girls, it went viral and crazy, and we had to leave our house. Dr Phil and Oprah on the doorstep. It was just one of those things. My husband worked for World of Dance and they do a lot more hip-hop type things, so they needed an interval act and he said, 'My daughter and her little group could do it'. Lo and behold, someone videoed it and it went online. They were wearing two pieces, which isn't the norm in the non-dance world, and they were really good, but hip circling to the floor! Everyone went crazy! We got a bunch of negative stuff and went on *Good Morning America* to explain why we needed two pieces; we need to see their muscles etc. The public saw what they wanted to see. It became so negative and it was all over the Internet so we were getting a lot of negative popularity and so we hired a lawyer and got as much down as we could. The group ended up splitting up; it became toxic between them. The Single Ladies' Moms is what my friend wrote and based *Dance Moms* on.

I thought 'viral' meant being sick, eight years ago the Internet was different. We have a dance studio on our third level where Autumn used to go freestyle and we started a channel for our family for fun! And the positivity began. Autumn's freestyle channel started off and then when people saw that I taught it, they said why don't I do one. So Trick Tip Thursday came around a year later and then who knew what YouTube was going to be like today! A full circle from negativity to positivity.

Who inspires you?

A – I get this question a lot. I have a lot of people inspire me; it's like the whole entire world! Everybody! All my dance teachers, everyone who is above me, seeing the older dancers, all the kids that support me and those that I teach.

What piece of advice would you give young dancers?

A – Take every opportunity! Maybe there's a class you really don't want to take, but that's the one that's going to make you a better dancer! Always taking every chance that you have, not giving up on anything, not getting too hard on yourself and always looking forward to something. I'm a perfectionist and hard on myself, I need to listen to my own advice! Always enjoy the little moments with your friends; you're not going to remember who won first at the competition!

With Alexander Campbell

Alexander Campbell

I was lucky enough to secure an interview with Alexander Campbell after watching him pirouette immeasurably at the Royal Opera House in a pre-performance class.

Originally from Sydney, Australia, he began dancing quite young as it ran in his family, just as a hobby and alongside other sports. He didn't feel he was pushed into ballet; he believes he had a genuine interest. He has fond memories of his dance school where he trained for ten years; his teachers understood what he needed to develop and brought in many guest teachers. He joined the Royal Ballet School shortly after winning silver at the Genée International Ballet Competition and becoming a finalist at the world renowned Prix de Lausanne. Upon graduation he worked with Birmingham Royal Ballet before returning to London in 2011 for his debut as a first soloist for the Royal Ballet Company. His repertory with the company includes Basilio (*Don Quixote*), Lewis Carroll/White Rabbit and Magician/Mad Hatter (*Alice's Adventures in Wonderland*), Colas (*La fille mal gardée*), Bluebird and King Florestan (*Sleeping Beauty*), Hans-Peter/Nutcracker and Prince (*The Nutcracker*), Mercutio (*Romeo and Juliet*), to name just a few, although he remembers his very first role on the big stage whilst still at school, holding a candelabra!

Alexander is immensely humble for someone so talented and listening to his anecdotes of his memories of pirouette training, reminded me of some of the young dancers I teach!

Name – Alexander Campbell
Current title/Company – Principal Dancer, Royal Ballet Company
Training – The Royal Ballet School

What is your dance background?

I started ballet when I was about five or six, just as a hobby, once a week, for fun.

When did you move to the UK?

I moved to the UK when I was 16, just turned 16, to join the Royal Ballet School. So I trained in Australia privately for around ten years.

I heard your grandparents were in Ballet Rambert?

Yeah they were, in the fifties, that's where they met! My parents didn't really dance though. My mum took classes when she was a child and my dad was a cricketer, so I have a bit of sporting background.

What do you remember from your training of pirouettes? What was focused upon?

I had access to a lot of teachers growing up, I did ballet, I did jazz, I did character. I don't really remember anything specific in terms of technique or about the positioning, but I just remember turning a lot! Especially in the character classes, the teacher I had was quite excited to, one, have a boy in the class and one who had some ability! And we used to do all sorts of turns, from the corner firstly, not necessarily pirouettes from fourth or anything, like chassé coupe chassé, both sides, right and left, just down the diagonal and she really made me do them superfast, and that's something that I remember doing a lot of. Oh and I remember my teacher making me hold a character shoe as my arms never made it close enough!

Do you remember how old you were when you first started pirouettes?

I think I was probably, maybe, seven or eight, doing my first classical pirouette. I may have done the other stuff with the Russian teacher before that but I remember the 'point, tendu, try and do a pirouette', which was horrible. I don't think I actually turned!

Are there any day-to-day factors that affect the efficiency of your turns? Some dancers like to say 'Today isn't a turning day'.

It's probably more how I'm feeling physically. I've got a bit of problem with my left knee and my left big toe, so if I'm turning on my right and I've had a particularly big day the day before and I'm a bit sore and stiff, my demi-pointe isn't so stable, so that would maybe affect it. Other things… I think if my hips are tight, and it's hard to get my hips level, that would really throw me off.

When I watched the Royal Ballet class, I noticed you drew your arms in from á la seconde to en avant throughout the turn. Is this something you do to help speed, or to do more turns?

I didn't realise I do that! I think it allows me to keep a good consistent pace and also allows me to alter the pace depending on what I am doing. If I need to do it quickly I will pull them in. I think in a class situation I'm trying to keep in control, especially if it is in an exercise needing harder pirouettes.

Young dancers find spotting quite hard. What do you think about when you spot or do you have any tips for them?

I think spotting is really good, but me personally, I don't think I am a great spotter; it's not something that I really think of! I'm very aware of what is going on around me as I'm turning, but I'm not focused on one particular thing. Although if I'm having a bad day, I will think about that and it does help. The best turns I do are when I'm thinking about turning with my shoulders and my neck is quite relaxed, and then I can adjust to what is going on, as opposed to being too focused on one place.

Every little dancer wants a TurnBoard! Have you had a go on one of these?

Well, we had one at school, although not in class of course. It was just something to mess around on in the common room. They don't really help turns, as your weight is in the wrong place. The first couple of times I tried I thought, 'Gosh why can't I do this?' Then I sat my weight back and there we go! It's spinning, not really turning. If you prepare too hard too, you just fall over! There were some pretty spectacular falls!

How many pirouettes is your big total?

I did ten once, which was fun! I haven't done that for a while though! Not 55 like Sophia Lucia, I don't even know how she does that, I saw it and I watched it, and I can't work it out! It's amazing! I don't know how you keep that going; I'm fascinated to find out! I suppose you have less friction in a tap shoe! A friend of mine trained in the USA and in a lot of acrobatics. I had some of the children there for private lessons and they're so strong from their acro core work, as well as having no fear. All of them can spin, and spin hard, four or five turns at the age of five! Would love to know how!

Would you say you're a natural turner?

Look, I enjoyed it when I was young, so I did it a lot, so it became natural. It's one of those things that if you do it a lot, a lot of practising, it becomes more natural.

Are you a righty or a lefty?

I naturally would turn to the left as a kid, I just always would spin that way, but then I came to the school, we had to turn to the right and that's the way it was. Most of the time now I will turn to the right, so I'm fairly even, it's cool to be able to do that!

With Gabriela Banuet

Sophia Lucia's Instagram first exposed this amazing lady to me. After seeing some Pilates-based photos on both Sophia's and Kalani's (*Dance Moms*) Instagram accounts, I had to have a little sneak at her profile. Gabby uses such an intricate selection of tools and exercises to activate many micro muscles in the dancers' bodies. It just so happens that her main hub was right around the corner from Master Ballet Academy so I was

Gabriela Banuet

able to coordinate and share ideas with her on my trip to Arizona. She also put Sam through his paces at her studio; it was awesome to see her in action!

Name – Gabriela Banuet
Current title/Company – Master Pilates and conditioning trainer. Founder of Intense Dancers Project and Gabriela Banuet Method
Training – Dance then fitness with Pilates-style personal training and functional stretch release

What is your background?

I've been dancing for a long time; I started dancing when I was five. But I was always really curious as to how the body works. I only had the information that my teachers gave me; I was thirsty to learn more and more and more. I have always been fascinated by the body, anatomy is my number one. Then I decided to do a training certification; the more I understood how the body functioned the more I wanted to learn. The only method that I found similar to dance when I couldn't dance any more was Pilates. I felt like I was doing the same technique with alignment and I felt so good about it. One day I thought if I implement everything of Pilates in every move we dance; it led to what I am doing right now! I also took some Tai Chi classes, bringing the energy in and drawing it back out connects so perfectly to dancers.

What is important for you in turns?

A turn is a lot. It's so much information!

The most important part for me in a turn, more than bringing awareness or connection, alignments, it's about feeling it. Because every turn has to be planned it has to be a take-off, it's not just spinning. I say no carousels and no Tasmanian devils! There is a difference between spinning and turning! So I always tell my kids, it's a feeling; you have to acknowledge everything, especially your force and resistance with the connections. Here comes one of my stories, I call my turns, 'turnados'!

Where does the tornado come from, the sky or Mother Earth? So Mother Earth decides to put some force to start the tornado coming and spinning into the top. So the alignment in the centre, the hole of the tornado, isn't a hole, but it is the force that creates and surrounds the turn. It depends how strong your tornado is! So the top of the tornado, if you don't have a solid connection that tornado is going to explode, so you have to keep the connection with the tornado in the core but also strong on the top. But at the same time, the tornado recycles the energy. Dynamic strength in the position, not static, the force goes down to go back up again and does not to keep the power on the outside but on the inside.

I can grab a bowl with icing. Where is the best place to hold the spatula to get the best whipped icing; at the bottom? No, your hands get sticky! At the very top? No, it won't get any whip. But hold it in the middle and the icing whips up with a strong force.

Another way I approach my turns is connecting it to a blender – there has to be a connection to the plug to get force into the blender, the lunge is the plug, the floor is the socket... but I'm not going to give you all my secrets!

For more information on Gabriela's techniques follow Intense Dancers Project on social media @intensedancersproject.

With Indiana Woodward

Indianna Woodward

You can always trust that a ballet company will have an array of dancers from many different countries and backgrounds. All of them have had different styles of ballet training before they embark on their full-time training, often with the School of American Ballet, which is affiliated with NYCB.

Upon reading a programme whilst sitting at the Lincoln Center, Indiana's array of countries jumped out at me... Born in Paris, but trained in California with a Russian teacher and then moved to NYC. I thought if I had the chance to chat to her, her stories for pirouettes would be exciting to have as part of the book. Luckily the NYCB Press Office returned my email... and the rest is below!

Name – Indiana Woodward
Current title/Company – New York City Ballet – Corps de Ballet
Training – Yuri Grigoriev School of Ballet in Venice, California and School of American Ballet

What is your dance background?

I was trained by Yuri Grigoriev, who was located in Venice, California. I studied with him for about six years. He is completely Russian trained and from the Stanislavsky, so he trained us that way. Then I won a prize to go to the Bolshoi Academy in Russia to study and perform with the school for two months when I was 15. Then I studied at the School of American Ballet in New York City for two years before getting into New York City Ballet.

What do you remember from your training of pirouettes? What was focused upon?

Pirouette in a Russian technique is quite different from Balanchine. The Russian technique enforces taking off for a pirouette from a stable two-legged fourth position. I also remember having a little bit more of a crossed passé, which helps to put you on your exact axis. The arm position was also a little different, a straight front arm and side arm as well (which is different from RAD training). I found that I could turn many times using this technique. Then I developed my dance career further and learnt the Balanchine technique. To take off from a pirouette you must stretch and straighten the back leg on the floor behind you far enough that you feel more weight on the front leg. With the same type of arms from the Russian technique, straight to the front and side, you take off and it works just as well and even sometimes more consistently. I remember the teacher explaining that if you stretched everything out correctly and go down to go up, it gives you the most exciting and controlled look. It also helps to have a big Balanchine fourth because right from the beginning it gets you on your front leg.

Do you remember how old you were when you first started pirouettes?

I think I may have been around eight or so when we first learned baby turns, maybe younger but can't remember those years.

Are there any day-to-day factors that affect the efficiency of your turns? Some dancers like to say 'Today isn't a turning day'.

I think the day-to-day factors may be a mental thing for the most part, but there are definitely days when my shoes don't have a good platform to turn on or have little bumps from the glue in the tip, or the ground you're turning on may have a bump or thick tape.

Young dancers find spotting quite hard. What do you think about when you spot or do you have any tips for them?

Spotting is definitely a difficult thing. I would give the advice of just extremely committing to focusing on one thing. To really look at the thing and engage your eye focus on it. That helps me turn my head faster as well.

Who is your inspiration?

I have so many people who inspire me. I would say a lifelong inspirational person would be Sylvie Guillem because I find her entire journey so incredible, as well as Alina Cojocaru. Also I am truly inspired every day by my fellow colleagues of the New York City Ballet. Every single dancer here is extremely talented and brings such different qualities to the company.

With Lulu Alexandra

As both an ice skater and a dancer, I was really interested to see some comparisons and differences between the two techniques. Lulu shared with me some information about her career and how she turns.

Name – Lulu Alexandra www.lulualexandra.com
Current title/Company – Professional performer and competitive ice skater
Training – Mountview Conservatoire and Arts Educational School, London
Russian Master Skating Coach – Viktor Teslia

At what age do young ice skaters begin their training for turning?

We start spinning as soon as we have the confidence. I tried on my very first go, aged six.

Do ice skaters spot when they turn like dancers? And if not how do you not get dizzy?

We don't spot – we go too fast and it would be impossible. However, when I was at Arts Ed, I found not spotting easier and I could easily do six clean turns. When I learned spotting, I only ever really managed three, four on a good day.

Skaters are only required to spin one way, whereas in dance you must turn both ways. Most skaters spin in a forwards direction on their left leg and backwards on their right. However, I do all mine back to front! We don't get dizzy because generally you build up speed etc. with skill, so the speed increases over time. Sometimes things can affect this – spinning at altitude, when tired or having a cold can make it feel quite nasty...

When turning on ice what are your biggest focuses?

Good spinning requires a strong core before anything, regardless of the positions. The layback and cannonball require extra skill, as putting your head down or back whilst spinning is ultra-disorientating.

Research has been done into why skaters don't get dizzy and it seems to be down to training the brain to right itself.

Having said that, I have suffered from vertigo due to over-spinning over many years and if you research 'Lucinda Ruh vertigo', you should find some interesting information on some of the perils involved in spinning (Lucinda was an exceptional spinner but has suffered years of vertigo since).

7. ENDNOTE
FROM MYRA TIFFIN, *FISTD, ARAD*

Coming to the end of this book and having sat engrossed reading it on a long flight to Canada there is one word that springs to mind. Brilliant. Such an informative book that makes total sense, not only to the experienced dance teacher, but with light-hearted twists and personal references, will capture and inspire young students to push forward with the satisfaction of achieving consistency and accuracy in their turns.

Whilst reading the book many flashbacks of my own professional training under the outstanding, unique guidance of Noreen Bush, FRAD, sprung to mind. Remembering classes where Miss Bush would stand right in front of me and state in her formidable style, 'Now turn!' Fear ran through every part of your body and the worry of smacking your terrifying principal around the face ensured you achieved the turn. The tools and imagery used within this book can all be cross-referenced to what I was being made to do, 40 years ago. I became a natural turner without fully understanding how. This book has answered all those questions and many more. Before going to full-time college I had grown up believing that 'it's not your day for turning' so accepted that was why I very rarely managed a double! How wrong I was when someone actually taught me how to do it. My record for fouetté turns was 42 on pointe commenced with a double pirouette and consistently turned five turns in pirouette exercises. Looks as if pirouettes run in the blood.

Rosina's understanding of turning is so clearly and eloquently explained in this book, and together with it being technically proven on my students, Pirouette Surgery® is a recipe for success.

I cannot wait for what Rosina has next, watching her change the UK's teaching methods one by one. I have seen first hand how her methods have elevated my students' technique, skills and artistry in many different parts of their training.

ACKNOWLEDGEMENTS

With thanks to:

Sophia Lucia, Jaclyn Lucia and DBA Talent

Master Ballet Academy and Slawomir Woźniak

Autumn and Krista Miller and their team at Go 2 Talent

Alexander Campbell and the Royal Ballet Company

Indiana Woodward and the New York City Ballet Press Office

Bailey Callahan and the Radio City backstage tour experience

Samuel Downing Personal Training; endless cups of tea and unfaltering support

Jim Taylor and Joy Hewitt

Gabriela Banuet

Lulu Alexander

Gillian Murphy – ABT

Robert Skears with Shotz4U Photography

Andy Caballero Salcido – For your perfect cover design

Dancers from Myra Tiffin Performing Arts School: especially my models Darcie, Lily and Lauren

Fink's Salt and Sweet – N4 and Nanna's – N1 for flat whites on tap and too much cake

BIBLIOGRAPHY

Krasnow, D. MS, M., Wilmerding, V. PhD, Stecyk, S. PhD, ATC, CSCS, Wyon, M. PhD, and Koutedakis, Y. PhD, Biomechanical Research in Dance: A Literature Review 2011

Bronner, S., Brownstein, B. A kinematic analysis of the passé in skilled dancers [abstract]. J Dance Med Sci 1998;2(4)149.

Sandow, E., Bronner, S., Spriggs, J., Bassile, C. C., Rao, A. K. A kinematic comparison of a dance movement in expert dancers and novices [abstract]. J Orthop Sports Phys Ther 2003;33(2):A-25.

Laws, K. An analysis of turns. Dance Res J 1978–79;11/1–2:12–19.

Laws, K. The mechanics of the fouetté turn. Kinesiol Dance. 1986;28(4):22–24.

Laws, K. L. An analysis of turns. Dance Res J 1978–79;11/1–2:12–19.

Laws, K., Fulkerson, L. The slowing of Pirouettes. Kinesiology Med Dance 1992/1993;15(1 Fall/Win):72–80.

Lott, Melanie B., Laws, Kenneth L. The Physics of Toppling and Regaining Balance during a Pirouette. (2012) Journal of Dance Medicine & Science, 16(4), p.167.

Sugano, A., Laws, K. Physical analysis as a foundation for Pirouette training. Med Probl Perform Art 2002;17(1):29–32.

Meglin, J., Woollacott, M. The neural choreography underlying a pirouette-arabesque. Kinesiology Med Dance 1992;14:95–

Wilson, M., Kwon, Y. (2008). The Role of Biomechanics in understanding dance movement. *Journal of Dance Medicine & Science*, 12(3).

Kwon, Y. (2009). Study of dance in the mechanical perspective: dance biomechanics. Korean J Dance, 9, pp.124-130.

Hargrove, T., Hargrove, T. (2010). Five Misconceptions About Posture. [online] Better Movement by Todd Hargrove. Available at: http://www.bettermovement.org/blog/2010/five-misconceptions-about-posture

Thehealthydancer.blogspot.co.uk. (2013). The Healthy Dancer: Spotting & Why It Works. [online] Available at: http://thehealthydancer.blogspot.co.uk/2013/06/spotting-why-it-works.html

Pappas, S. (2016). Why Kids Love Getting Dizzy. [online] Braindecoder. Available at: https://braindecoder.com/post/why-kids-love-getting-dizzy-1251740214

Prevost, N. (2016). The Sound of a Pirouette and Tips on Mastering Multiples. [online] Danceadvantage.net. Available at: http://www.danceadvantage.net/multiple-Pirouettes/ [Accessed 24 May 2016].

Bushman, Barbara A. *ACSM's Resources For The Personal Trainer*. 4th ed. Lippincott

Jensen, R. K. (1981) The effect of a 12-month growth period on the body moments of inertia of children. Med Sci Sports Exerc 13: 238-242.

Yosmaoğlu, H. (2015). *Proprioception - The forgotten sixth sense*. Foster City, USA: Omits Groups Ebooks, p.2.

INDEX

A

Á la secondes   161-166

Abdominals   40, 110-118

Acceleration   18, 25-26, 32, 34, 72

Adductors   30, 110

Alexander Campbell   72, 102, 154, 193-197

American Ballet Theatre   131

Angular Velocity   33-34, 72

Ankle

    Alignment   40, 43, 86-88, 100, 156

    Imagery   86, 157

    Strength   86

Arms

    Importance of   24, 34, 39, 42, 45-47, 56, 60-80, 101-102, 154, 185-186, 189, 194, 202

    Imagery   149

Positions   67-68

Autumn Miller   46, 143, 167, 180-192

B

Balance   31-34, 44-46, 54-55, 101, 107, 120, 129-131, 133, 135, 183

Beach ball   57, 186

Biomechanics
 What is 30-31, 61
 Scientific studies 47-49
Breathing 112, 125-126, 182
Bulking 93-94

C

Centre of Gravity 32-33, 95, 98-99, 158-159, 161
Centrifugal Force 23, 63-64
Centripetal Forces 63-64
Chaînés 167
Changing Spot 137
Clapping 156
Core 40, 110-118
 Strengthening exercises 113-118
Counterbalance 85, 161

D

Dance Science 30-32
Dance Moms 7, 175
Dizziness 121, 129-130

F

Feet 102
Fifth line 119
Fondu 84- 85

Fouettés   61-166

G

Gabriela Banuet   60-61, 198-200
Gina Pero   157-158
Gluteals   82, 83, 88-91
        Strength exercises   91
Gymnastics   61, 186
        Rhythmic   22, 160
Gyrotonics®   119
Gyrokenisis®   119

H

Habits   152-157
Hairstyles   134
Hands   20, 71
Happy Knees   81-82

I

Ice-skating   46, 52,102-104, 204-205
Imagery   69, 124, 138, 148-151, 206
Indianna Woodward   201-203
Inertia   33-34, 42, 46, 49-50, 67, 72, 101-102, 160, 174,
Initial Reaction Phase   100
Instagram   26-27, 29, 77, 107, 109, 179, 181, 198
Invisible Muscle   57

J

Joy Hewitt   38
Jim Taylor   38

K

Kinematic processes   31
Kinetic processes   31
Knees   81-82, 98, 107
Krista Miller   51, 60, 162, 180-192

L

Latissimus Dorsi   40, 57, 70-71, 75, 117, 144
Leg Grabs   160
Leg
    Placement   81-86, 88-03
    Strength   88-93
Lulu Alexandra   104, 204-205

M

Magnet Hands   71
Master Ballet Academy   12-13
Matt Mattox   64
Mikhail Baryshnikov   42-43
Myosource   92-93
Myra Tiffin   206

N

Nathan Prevost   42-43

New York   8

O

Obliques   111, 117, 182

P

Pace   72-73, 154, 194

Pelvic Floor   112

PEP   8

Plank   115-118, 183

Plié   39-40, 189

Plunging Lunge   15, 46, 158

Pointe   20-21, 23-24, 159

Posè Turns   166

Position   53-59

Posture   39, 49, 54-55, 59,64, 76-78, 86, 89, 107-112, 115, 126, 174

Preparation   17-18, 32, 39-41, 48, 62-63, 88, 95-106, 153, 158-159, 161-163, 185

Proprioceptive System   129-130, 173

Props   57, 78-79, 136, 155

Q

Quadriceps   81, 88-89, 93, 96

R

Rachel Sebastian   16
Radio City Rockettes   123
Rake   161
Rhythm   123-131, 135, 153-154, 162, 185

S

Samuel Downing   61, 70, 74-75, 88,
Seat Belt   52, 56, 62-63,
Sophia Lucia   7, 12-29 43-44, 46, 99, 109, 120, 143, 196, 198
Sound Effects   127
Spinning   7, 46, 59 68-69, 120-122, 140, 148, 150, 188, 196, 199
        204-205
Spinning tops   51, 69
Spine   107-118, 126, 134
Spotting   48, 123, 125, 129-142, 154, 156, 182-184, 195, 203-204
        Imagery   138-139
        Training   138-139
Stairway to Pirouettes   152

T

T.Rex   60, 66
The Clock Game   139, 142, 49, 62
Torque   31-32, 34, 39-40, 82, 88, 97, 102, 104, 111, 154, 159, 162
Transverse Abdominis   59, 110-112
Travelling Turns   166-167

Trunk   40, 111, 126, 173-174
Turnboard   28, 122, 144, 196

V

Velocity   33-34, 46, 62, 72, 74, 84, 143
Vestibular System   107, 120-121, 129-130, 140
Visual System   130

W

Whiplash   135
Wind up   62, 80, 101, 185
Wings   57, 59, 70-71
World Record   12, 18-19
Workshops   8, 123, 178